The Silver Spoon

Recipes for Babies

Introduction

Food is essential to living well. It provides the necessary nutrition for life, but food is also a source of pleasure. From the earliest possible moment, it is crucial to teach infants how to eat well and enjoy trying new foods, making sure they are set on a path towards appreciating mealtimes and making healthy choices. This is achievable with a little planning, even if you are a busy parent with a hectic schedule.

We cannot take our children's attitude to food for granted, especially when it comes to vegetables and fruit. Raising a child to enjoy real food in a world of processed snacks is a challenge that every parent faces. By the word "parent", we mean anyone who is responsible for the wellbeing of a child and so the terms "primary care-giver" or "carer" may be used instead.

Traditionally, Italian children sit at the table with the adults and eat everything from anchovies to artichokes. Italian parents pass a love of seasonal foods down to their children, and this generational appreciation of good food has made Italy the culinary center we know today.

Italian is one of the most popular cuisines in the world, but what is it that makes it so universally appealing to adults and children alike? Over the centuries, Italians have learnt how to mix a few simple, good-quality ingredients together to make healthy meals that are full of flavor.

The Italian way of eating, as epitomized by **The Silver Spoon**, promotes family mealtimes— everyone sitting down together and sharing food and conversation. This is positive as infants copy the behavior of siblings and parents.

The Silver Spoon is the best-selling cookbook found in almost every Italian family's kitchen. It is full of traditional recipes that have been handed down from generation to generation. With any cookbook from **The Silver Spoon**, you can imagine that you are in a home kitchen learning how to cook the Italian way.

All the recipes in **The Silver Spoon: Recipes for Babies** have been double-tested by an expert nutritionist and are devised to safely wean your baby onto solid foods from the age of six months onwards. Home-cooked baby foods provide the reassurance that you know exactly what your child is eating. Jars of baby puree are convenient and have their place, but are best reserved for those moments when you are out and about, traveling, or simply do not have the time to cook from scratch.

None of the recipes in this book are particularly time consuming to make and many can be cooked in larger batches and frozen. Whenever possible, keep life simple by cooking for yourself at the same time as for your child. Often you do not have to cook a piece of meat or fish separately for your baby—instead, save a slice of roast chicken, lamb, or beef from your family meal, making sure that you do not season the meat during cooking, and blend it into a puree.

Setting your child on the path to enjoying vegetables and fruit as an infant, will serve them well throughout their life. Instead of being seen as something we eat when we are being "good" or on a health kick, enjoying vegetables and fruit should be integral to children's lives— something they do automatically, with as much pleasure as grabbing a sweet treat.

Although the advice in this book has in some cases been revised for a non-Italian readership, it was originally written from the point of view of an Italian family and is intended to show you how Italian babies and children are given the gift of a life-long love of a wide variety of foods and flavors. A well-balanced diet is one of the keys to good nutrition, but equally important is your general approach to food and eating. If the entire family embraces the idea that food is to be enjoyed and shared, your child is likely to have this healthy attitude to food as well.

Introduction

Recipe symbols

gluten-free

dairy-free

vegan

vegetarian

suitable for refrigeration

suitable for freezing

Getting organized

Creating a baby-friendly kitchen

Feeding needs to be an enjoyable experience for parents and baby alike. Those who gain pleasure from food during mealtimes throughout their childhood have fewer problems keeping up a healthy diet as an adult and are less likely to develop issues around food. The setting for this formative food experience is the kitchen, which must become a welcoming place for every baby.

Making small changes

Whether tiny or spacious, old-fashioned or high-tech, once a child appears on the scene, it's a good idea to organize even the smallest of kitchens to suit the needs of the entire family. There is no need to unleash an army of architects to knock down walls or employ interior decorators to rearrange furniture. Actually, just a few changes are needed to create a safe and tranquil corner where parents and baby can embark on their new adventure in feeding, together creating a unique bond in the process.

Setting the scene

Grown-ups love to eat their food in a quiet, dimly lit, ambient atmosphere. For a baby, it is enough simply not to have bright lights shining in their face as they savor their first spoonfuls of grated apple or pear. In reality, little effort is needed to turn part of the kitchen into a calm oasis for the new bonding experience between parent and baby that occurs during feedtime.

Keeping baby happy

In the early months, breast or bottle feeding can be done in a comfortable nursing chair, as part of the nursery furniture. When the time comes to start weaning, switch to a high chair, which keeps a baby upright while feeding and eliminates the risk of choking. Find a space for the high chair near the adults' table where it can be positioned safely and conveniently to offer food to the baby, whose first experiences of pureed fruit, pureed vegetables, or baby rice work best when everyone feels relaxed, comfortable, and well-disposed in a comfortable chair.

Important features of a high chair

At mealtimes the high chair should be strategically placed in the dining area where it isn't too busy and away from very bright lights. If the high chair is in the kitchen, it should be away from the heat of a stove or oven.

A high chair needs to:
· conform to strict guaranteed safety standards: look for the seal of approval from the Consumer Product Safety Commission in the US or the Kitemark in the UK, which means it is approved by the British Standards Institution
· be stable and impossible to topple over
· be light and easy to carry
· be convenient to store
· be easy to clean
· be the right size for your baby, so trying it out first in-store is a good idea
· have an adjustable seat height, so it can grow with your child

It is recommended that you never leave a child in a high chair unattended. If you have to move away from your baby for a few seconds, place the high chair with its back to a wall to be certain it will not topple over.

Harnessing the power of kitchen appliances

Now it's time to turn your attention to the kitchen appliances. First in line is the refrigerator and freezer. There's no need to change them for newer models, however a quick reorganization is an excellent idea.

Reorganizing the refrigerator

In homes without babies, the refrigerator and freezer are often a refuge for small portions of leftovers, which are always handy to snack on after a hard day's work, or a treasure trove of tempting ingredients that can be quickly thrown together and put on the table for a dinner with friends. Follow the manufacturer's advice for keeping the refrigerator at the optimum temperature for storing food and also for keeping everything scrupulously clean using hot, soapy water. When refrigerating leftovers, make sure they are cool before putting into the refrigerator and either store the food in an airtight container or covered in plastic wrap.

Make good use of the freezer

The freezer will be your friend when it comes to making and storing baby cereals and purees. There are a few basic recipes, such as vegetable broth (see page 58) and pureed vegetables (see page 64), that are heavily relied on during weaning; these recipes are handy to make in large batches, stored in the freezer in individual portions and taken out as needed. Frozen foods are a safe alternative to freshly prepared foods approved by even the strictest pediatricians.

Turning on the oven

Once baby arrives, the oven becomes an essential piece of equipment for the parent-turned-cook during the months just after weaning. Aside from steaming, roasting and baking in the oven are recommended methods of cooking for infants, particularly after the first 12 months. The oven can be used for roasting fish and meat that can then be pureed, as well as baking baby-friendly cookies (see page 156).

Taking advantage of the microwave

Often used reluctantly as a time-saving measure when cooking, the microwave can be a real help once the baby arrives. The microwave is a useful kitchen aid for parents, and is handy for quickly cooking fruit and vegetables that can then be made into purees. For warming formula, however, it is best to heat feeding bottles in a pan of warm water to avoid overheating. Likewise, for warming purees, it is preferable to gently heat the food in a small pan rather than using a microwave. Food warmed in a microwave does not always heat evenly and can have "hot spots" that are a potential scalding risk if not stirred thoroughly.

No matter what method you use to warm your baby's meal, always check the temperature of the food before giving it to your child.

Small but essential kitchen utensils

Despite the many different preparations carried out in the kitchen, there are actually very few really essential utensils.

Measuring

When following any recipe, you need to measure out the ingredients. A set of digital kitchen scales is useful for weighing dry ingredients, but for liquids, a measuring cup or measuring jug is a simple solution. The quantity of each ingredient in all the recipes that follow within this book are given in US cups, metric, and also imperial. Choose your preferred system, and follow that one set of measurements throughout.

Mixing

A stainless steel or silicone whisk keeps lumps from forming when adding baby rice or instant cereal to a broth (stock). Another time-saving utensil is a silicone or rubber spatula, known as a scraper, used to empty out pans and bowls.

Cutting

A multipurpose knife is sufficient for slicing vegetables, but more proficient cooks prefer to use a chef's knife. The curved blade allows you to chop all kinds of ingredients without using the traditional mezzaluna chopper.

Cooking

Bearing in mind the amounts of vegetable broth (stock), steamed and pureed vegetables, and simple soups that new parents prepare in the early months, the minimum requirements for cooking are a pan with a lid for boiling, a saucepan for warming single portions of food, and a steamer basket for cooking vegetables, meat, and fish.

Pureeing and straining

During weaning, blending ingredients to a smooth puree is the first step in the preparation of solid food. For this, you will need a hand-held immersion (stick) blender or food processor. The traditional food mill, which grinds the fibers in food when you turn the handle, can also be used, but these days electric blenders and processors are preferred for convenience. Of course, cooked vegetables should be pureed after being drained using a slotted spoon or after the broth (stock) has been filtered through a fine-mesh strainer.

Grating and juicing

A hand grater is useful for grating a pear or an apple; this can be safely used and cleaned in a flash. For juicing, the best gadget to have is a countertop electric juicer but you can also use a hand-held immersion (stick) blender for purees and smoothies.

Babies under the age of 12 months do not need fruit juice; other than milk, water is the best drink. If you do chose to give fruit juice to your baby after six months, once solids have been introduced, it must be diluted ten parts water to one part juice.

A new way to shop

When infants are present in the home, issues around the origins and safety of food become a priority. Where to shop for food, how to assess the quality of produce, and which products to trust are some of the questions that parents are likely to ask. Here are a few simple guidelines.

Always buy fresh fruit and vegetables

With the arrival of a baby, you will need to make sure that the fruit and vegetables you feed your baby should be as fresh as possible. To ensure this, it is necessary to restock fresh produce frequently, ideally every few days. But where can you shop with confidence? With the arrival of their first child, many new parents turn to organic food stores. That's one option. However, it is also possible to find a reliable supply of good-quality fruit and vegetables at your local market, grocer or supermarket. When shopping, learn to trust your own senses.

The importance of freshness

Always choose fresh produce that is in season and grown within the country you live in or, even better, from the areas of production closest to your home. If this is not always possible, simply choose the produce that looks freshest with no bruises, soft spots, or wilting.

As you become more familiar with fresh produce, fruit and vegetables will start to "speak to you." If a zucchini (courgette) is plump, whole, and bright green, then the chances are that it is also excellent to eat. Particularly during the height of the growing season. In this case, it is enough to wash, peel, and cook the vegetables as indicated in the recipe.

But then comes the ultimate test. By taste alone, you can determine whether you have bought good produce or whether you still have much to learn when shopping. At markets, you can learn a lot by observing the way more experienced shoppers deal with the traders.

Meat, fish, eggs, and cheese

When buying these food stuffs, chose the best quality as often as you can. From when you wean your baby to the age of 12 months, meat will mainly be given in pureed form with the gradual transition to a chunkier texture. When it comes to sourcing meat, it's a good idea to establish a trusting relationship with a butcher and ask questions about the origins of the meat when making your purchase. If you're shopping in supermarkets, try to buy the best quality.

Freshness is of paramount importance when buying fish. Whenever you're in doubt or unfamiliar with this kind of purchase, frozen fish is a really good alternative.

For cheese and eggs, the advice is to read the labels carefully. Only feed a baby cheese made from pasteurized milk. Do not give them mould-ripened cheese, such as Brie or Camembert, or soft blue-veined cheese, such as Roquefort, unless fully cooked as these types of cheese can harbor listeria.

Always chose the highest quality eggs you can afford. In the UK, an egg stamped with the Red Lion Mark and with British Lion Quality on the carton has been produced to the highest standards. When buying eggs without such a mark, always buy them from a trusted supplier.

Getting organized

Fresh is best

Always read the label

At larger stores and supermarkets, the label on a food item allows you to determine the origin of the produce and check its best-before date. Nonetheless, after the initial moments of uncertainty, the untrained eye of the parent soon learns to spot just the right piece of lean, tender meat for their infant. Getting into the habit of checking the appearance of all produce at the same time as reading the label helps when appraising the quality of food.

Freeze if you can

Frozen food products are the only safe alternative to fresh produce approved by pediatricians, particularly when feeding your baby with vegetables that are not in season, such as peas, spinach, and pumpkin.

The same goes for fish. It's better to use a safe frozen product than an unfrozen fish whose freshness cannot be guaranteed.

Freezing food at home is also great for storing large batches of cooked food. Most purees freeze really well. Cool any food quickly that is going to be frozen and always label the container with the contents and date.

Ready-to-use products

When it comes to shop-bought purees, instant baby rice and cereals, sugar-free teething biscuits (rusks), and soup pasta or other small pasta shapes, you can relax. All the large baby food manufacturers sell products that are highly controlled and safe to eat. Cartons of fruit juice, however, are not recommended, despite being convenient and safe, babies do not need to drink juice. It is best to offer fruit purees when you want them to have something sweet, ideally made at home from fresh seasonal fruit.

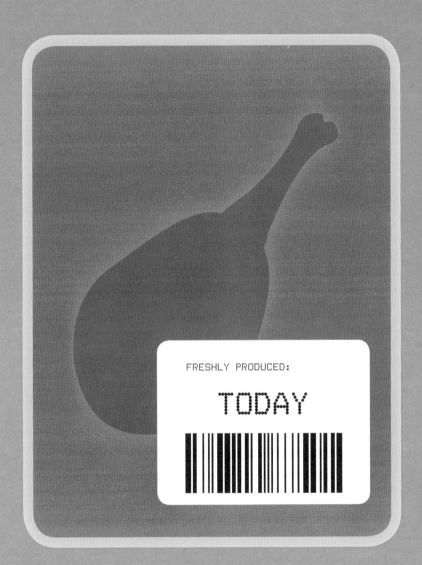

FRESHLY PRODUCED:

TODAY

Keeping a well-stocked pantry

The advantage of keeping a well-stocked, neatly organized pantry is that you only need to restock those items that you use regularly a couple of times each month. With a little practice, it's possible to work out how much of any one food stuff you use each week and replace any less perishable items only occasionally, making sure to check their expiry dates on the label.

Cereals and soup pasta

In the first months of weaning, you should always have a small supply of baby rice, corn, or tapioca, and gluten-free cereal flour products, which are recommended until the seventh month. After this time, you can then gradually introduce gluten-containing wheat flour and soup pasta, which are small pasta shapes. Later on, it is useful to have larger pasta shapes too.

Teething biscuits

If you can find them, no-sugar teething biscuits (rusks) can be given to an infant as an occasional snack to munch on while sat in their high chair. However, most brands contain some sugar, in which case a breadstick, crust of bread, or a celery or carrot stick is a better option for a teething child.

Extra virgin olive oil

This condiment is recommended in Italy for use in the preparation of baby cereals because it is a healthy fat that also contains valuable antioxidants. Start by adding just a couple of drops. Italians believe that a kitchen should never be without it.

Dried legumes

Dried legumes (pulses) are only introduced at around the eighth month. From then on, it's a good idea to keep a supply of dried or canned garbanzo beans (chickpeas), beans, lentils, and peas in the cupboard. However, if you plan to use them in a soup or puree, any dried legume will need to be soaked in water overnight and so you may find canned pulses more convenient as they are ready to use and need no soaking. Be sure to check the label of any canned pulses to make sure they do not contain sugar.

Pureed baby food

There are all kinds of commercially available pureed baby foods. The most popular are those made from vegetables, fruit, and meat—first white meat, such as chicken, turkey, and then lamb and beef. If you choose to use ready-made baby food when first weaning your child, start by mixing a small amount with cereal dishes and gradually increase. Jars of pureed food can be convenient when you're short on time or traveling, but try not to rely on them too much. The best thing is to feed your baby fresh seasonal vegetables, fruit, and protein sources whenever you can.

The child-friendly refrigerator

Milk and yogurt

At the age of about six months, babies often transition from breast milk to formula, the choice of which is based on the specific needs of the child. Cows' milk should only be given to a child after 12 months. After this point, vegan infants may be weaned with full-fat soy milk that is fortified with calcium and vitamins B12 and D (other plant milks are much lower in protein than soy, so not suitable). Plain yogurt, which is a very popular choice for feeding infants, is good for mixing with pieces of fresh fruit. Kept in the refrigerator, a tub of plain yogurt can also be a great supply of calcium for a nursing mother.

Meat and ham

After the initial stage of feeding pureed meat to your baby, slices of fresh meat can be introduced into their diet. Meat should always be stored in the coldest part of the refrigerator and for no more than two or three days. Start by offering your child white meats, such as turkey and chicken, as they are more easily digested and contain less fat than red meat, but still contain a similar amount of iron. Once your baby has reached 12 months, you can begin to feed them a very small amount of lean cooked ham to vary the flavor of their food. Due to the high level of salt in ham, however, it must be gradually introduced.

Cheese

Small amounts of full-fat dairy products, such as plain yogurt and a little pasteurized cheese, can be introduced into their diet after the seventh month. For example, feed small amounts of cream cheese, cottage cheese, ricotta, or mozzarella. Similarly, a little hard cheese, such as Cheddar, Red Leicester, or Parmesan, can be added to meals and so it is useful to keep a stock in your refrigerator. These cheeses are high in protein that, thanks to the aging process that cheese undergoes, becomes easy to digest. Some hard cheeses can be high in salt, however, and so should be used in moderation. Full-fat cheeses and dairy products are recommended up to the age of two years, as young children need the energy from fats to help them grow.

Replenish fresh foods every few days

Fresh foods should only be bought in small quantities and then frequently restocked, depending on the shelf life of each food. Other foods last for longer in the refrigerator. The best-before date of a cheese, for example, is a reliable indication of the length of time a cheese can be kept.

Freezing food to save time

Home-freezing

A well-stocked freezer can provide a ready supply of handy, basic ingredients that, when thawed, enable you to quickly prepare lots of baby cereals and other nutritious dishes that are both healthy and delicious. For busy parents, freezing food at home is a time-saver approved by pediatricians.

Vegetable broth and meat broth

Vegetable broth (stock) is the basic ingredient for cooking any baby cereal. Making a large batch of broth and then freezing it in individual portions means that you will always have some ready to defrost whenever you need it. Preparing and freezing a vegetable broth is a good way to save time in the future. The same goes for the meat broth that is introduced into meals as your baby develops.

Pureed vegetables

The cooked vegetables that have been used to make a broth are then strained and pureed in either a food processor or with a hand-held immersion (stick) blender. They are then added to cereal during baby's first months. Pureed vegetables can easily be divided up into individual portions and stored in airtight containers in the freezer.

Fish

At those moments when you're unsure about the freshness of the fish on offer at your local market, instead buy frozen white fish fillets. Frozen fish is a useful freezer staple to have to hand for times you decide to make a cereal with fish after the eighth month. Always check any fish very carefully for small bones.

Fresh tomato sauce

At the height of the summer season, when tomatoes are at their best, make a sauce in large quantities and freeze it in individual portions. The sauce can then be used to flavor your baby's first pasta dishes or added to different preparations. A frozen tomato sauce is a convenient but healthy, tasty ingredient to have at the ready when you're short on time.

Vegetables and pulses

Although fresh is always best, frozen vegetables and pulses are approved by pediatricians as an excellent alternative when fresh vegetables are out of season. Peas and spinach, naturally stewed rather than sautéed in a skillet (frying pan), can be stocked in your freezer to be used at a later date and save time without sacrificing flavor and quality. Likewise, a soffritto—an aromatic mix of finely chopped onion, carrot, and celery that has been slowly fried in olive oil—can be frozen in batches to use as the base of a puree or broth.

A constant supply of fresh fruit and vegetables

Apples, pears, and bananas

The first fruit to be introduced into a baby's diet are apples, pears, and bananas. Always keep a few pieces of each in your fruit bowl. The secret to letting your baby appreciate fresh fruit, without the need for any added sugar, is to choose naturally sweet varieties such as Golden Delicious apples, Bosc pears, and very ripe bananas.

Oranges

The orange is one of the fresh fruit with the highest concentration of vitamin C, and can be given to infants as finger food in peeled segments after removing any pith and pips. Oranges come into season in winter, when there should always be a supply of them at home.

Potatoes, carrots, and zucchini

Potatoes, carrots, and zucchini (courgettes)—the main ingredients that make up a vegetable broth (stock)—are introduced gradually into a baby's diet, one by one. Just one month after weaning begins, however, they can be used together to make a broth. Once cooked, the vegetables can be pureed for use with cereal. A plentiful supply of these three vegetables is useful in the kitchen.

Squash

When boiled or steamed, squash or pumpkin is easy for infants to digest. Squash is also high in vitamin A, potassium, and minerals. You can buy squash while in season and it will then keep for a long time in the crisper drawer of the refrigerator. Raw pumpkin flesh can also be frozen.

White vegetables, green vegetables

White vegetables, such as celery stalks and fennel, have strong flavors. Although they are only used a little at a time, always have some ready to go in the refrigerator. Green vegetables, such as spinach, broccoli, and Swiss chard, are essential. First, they are added to a vegetable broth (stock) to add flavor but then strained and discarded. Later, the cooked green vegetables can be pureed and added to cereals.

Tomatoes

The tomato is among the most widely used ingredient. It's always best to use tomatoes when in season and when they are very ripe because they are easy to digest and higher in nutrients, such as vitamin C. Tomatoes are the main ingredient in tomato sauce, the first real condiment for pasta that is enjoyed by infants and grown-ups alike.

Healthy eating guidelines for babies and infants

Weaning

Weaning refers to the transition from a diet consisting exclusively of breast milk or formula milk to different solid foods. This transition should take place when milk or formula on its own is no longer sufficient to satisfy the nutritional needs of the infant, particularly energy, protein, iron, zinc, and vitamins.

Although the timing of weaning depends on the individual baby, scientific bodies generally agree on when it should begin. Weaning should ideally start around the sixth month, but not before the end of the fourth month. However, they do all recommend that, if possible, infants are breast fed exclusively until the age of six months.

How to introduce different foods

An infant is ready to receive solid food from six months onwards. At this stage, the child's intestines are fully developed and their neuro-logical development allows them to grasp, chew, and swallow solid food.

There are no prescribed instructions or set-in-stone menus with which to begin the weaning process. Different dietary patterns can allow the nutritional needs of a child to be met between the ages of six months and three years.

The process of weaning should encourage a baby to develop their own tastes and personal food choices from the perspective of a healthy diet, taking into account family food preferences, recommendations by pediatricians and health professionals, socio-cultural context, and local food traditions.

During weaning, foods can be given with a suitable size baby spoon. Alternatively, allow your baby to touch the food on the plate and eat it with their hands. Never force the infant to eat. If any food is rejected, you should not insist that baby eats it, but instead alternate different foods by color, flavor, and texture. Be patient. Any food initially rejected can be given again. If necessary, prepare the same food in a different way.

Between the ages of nine and 12 months, infants should try a wide variety of foods and flavors, as they gradually become accustomed to eating two main meals (lunch and dinner) and one or two snacks each day, alongside breast milk or formula. Portion sizes must be adjusted to suit the age and appetite of the child. Your baby's regular pediatrician or health visitor can offer good advice on how much to feed at each stage.

What can a baby eat after the age of 12 months?

Once babies reach 12 months, they are able to eat many of the things made for members of the family at large, provided the foods are prepared in such a way and with a consistency that facilitates chewing and swallowing, and without salt or sugar. However, even after 12 months babies still cannot be considered small adults and have specific nutritional needs that pediatricians will explain to parents.

A note on milk and water

Aside from breast milk or formula milk, babies must drink water when being weaned. Avoid drinks with added sugar, which can lead to tooth decay and obesity.

Getting organized

Breast milk – is the only food or drink babies need in the first six months of life. Once solid foods are introduced, ideally breast milk continues to be given alongside an increasingly varied diet. The World Health Organization recommends babies are breast fed for two years, if possible.

Formula milk – or first infant formula is usually based on cows' milk and is the only suitable alternative to breast milk for the first 12 months. In the UK, follow-on formula, while available, is generally not recommended for babies, unless under specific advice from a healthcare professional. Research has shown that there is no benefit in switching to follow-on formula at six months. First infant formula can be given up until your baby is 12 months old but is not needed beyond that age.

Cows' milk – must be pasteurized and can be used in cooking from six months, but it should not be given as a drink until 12 months. Use full-fat cows' milk for babies up to two years, as they need the extra energy and vitamins it contains. Semi-skimmed milk can be introduced at two years, as long as the child is a good eater with a varied diet.

Non-cows' milk or goats' milk formula – is produced to the same nutritional standards as cows' milk formula. It is no less likely to cause allergies in babies, however, and is not suitable for babies with a cows' milk protein allergy.

Only give soya formula or other formula milks for specific allergies or conditions when a healthcare professional advises you to do so.

Water – for babies under six months, boil tap water first and then leave it to cool. Bottled water is not recommended for making up formula as it contains too much salt (sodium) or sulphate. Do give your baby water to drink as soon solid foods are introduced into their diet.

The risk of allergies

If your baby already has an allergy, such as a diagnosed food allergy or eczema, or if there is a family history of food allergies, eczema, asthma, or hay fever, pay careful attention when introducing new foods. Talk to your family doctor or health visitor before weaning.

In order to spot any reaction, introduce new solid foods that may trigger allergies one at a time and only in very small amounts. These foods include cow's milk, eggs, nuts and seeds, soya, shellfish and fish, and foods containing gluten. Do not be tempted to cut out any major food, such as milk, because this can lead to your child not getting the nutrients they need.

Energy intake

A child's energy intake should be properly distributed among the macronutrients. For children aged between 12 months and three years, 50–55 percent should be derived from carbohydrates, 35–40 percent from fats, and about 10–15 percent from proteins. With regard to carbohydrates, it is advisable to restrict foods and beverages with added sugar.

Getting organized

Easy weaning

Moving on from the baby bottle

From the sixth month onwards, a baby needs more than milk. In order to grow, gain strength and be healthy, your baby requires solid food. After experimenting with baby rice or other cereals, purees of cooked vegetables and fruit, and sometimes raw fresh fruit, it is time to broaden your baby's diet to food with a more lumpy consistency. By the end of the twelfth month, their food should resemble proper meals.

How and when to start weaning

Weaning is when an exclusive diet of breast milk or formula milk makes way for new foods introduced through spoon-feeding. During this period, milk still makes up the greatest percentage of a baby's diet, but is gradually replaced by various foods during the first year.

Six months is the right age

Breast milk or formula provide the energy and nutrients your baby needs until six months old. After this age, an exclusive diet of breast milk or formula no longer satisfies an infant's nutritional requirements and may expose them to risks of protein imbalance, resulting from the uneven intake of fat; minerals such as iron, zinc, and calcium; and vitamins. All schools of pediatric thought consider that weaning should start between 17 weeks and 26 weeks.

Waiting until six months allows your baby to develop so they can cope with solid foods and are able to feed themselves. By this stage, the baby can move food around their mouth, chew, and swallow. They can stay in a seated position, hold their head, coordinate hands and mouth, pick up food and put it in their mouth, then swallow, rather than spit food back out.

If your baby was born prematurely, ask your health visitor or family doctor for advice on when to start introducing solid foods.

No forcing

Patiently coax your baby into trying new foods, but never force them to eat. When you first start weaning, it is a good idea to offer soft, bland food to ease the transition from milk to food. Offer a new vegetable or fruit puree every two to three days to introduce your baby to fresh flavors and prevent any problems with their digestion. When it comes to vegetables, starting with greener, less sweet ones is the latest recommendation to make it easier for baby to learn to like veg, but mashed cooked vegetables, like carrot, parsnip, and potato, along with rice, are great first foods. Cooked apple, or pear, or mashed banana can also be swiftly introduced. All of these foods will get your baby accustomed to the use of a spoon.

As a baby is still getting most of their energy and nutrients from breast milk or formula milk, do not worry about how much food they eat. It is more important to get them used to tastes and textures, and learn how to move solid foods around their mouth and swallow. Eating is a new skill. Some babies accept unfamiliar flavors and textures more quickly than others. Keep trying, giving lots of praise and encouragement.

Allow plenty of time for feeding. Go at your baby's pace and stop when they show you that they are full by firmly closing their mouth or turning their head away. Do not add sugar or salt to your baby's food or cooking water. Salt is not good for a baby's kidneys, while sugar may encourage a sweet tooth later in life.

Weaning from liquids to solids: start with milk and fruit

How to feed

For an infant's first contact with solid food, you can use any small spoon suited to the size of your baby's mouth. The spoon must be small enough to be inserted between the lips without triggering their tongue thrust reflex, which causes a baby to spit out things put into their mouth. Today there are very soft baby spoons made from silicone.

Do not add sugar or any sweetener to new foods in order to make the change from breast milk or formula to other foods "sweeter". This is a simple precaution to prevent infants from associating the new feeding spoon or implement with a particular sweet taste.

Fruit and milk-based products contain natural sugars and so your baby should find them sweet enough without the need to add any additional sugar. Introducing your child to too many sweet flavors early on may encourage them to develop a sweet tooth later in life.

Never add honey to your baby's food before the age of 12 months. Pediatricians recommend waiting until a child is at least 12 months before introducing honey as it may contain spores of bacteria that can cause botulism. This does not mean a supply of honey is contaminated and remember that these bacteria are harmless to adults and children over 12 months.

The gradual transition from liquid to solid

At the start of the weaning process, the new foods are likely to be more readily accepted when diluted, and with the little one sat in a comfortable position, seated in a high chair.

Serenity and tranquility are crucial ingredients for happy mealtimes. Any fear that the baby isn't eating enough or expectations of a difficult struggle to make them accept a new flavor will cause unnecessary problems that can be avoided. Trying new flavors and experimenting with different ways of eating should be a pleasure for any child.

The chart opposite is intended as a guide for babies aged six months. Babies have different dietary needs, depending on many factors, including their weight. Follow your baby's direction and initiative when deciding how much to feed them. For example, if towards the end of the first week of weaning you introduce a suppertime solid feed to your baby's routine only to find that they are too tired to eat, try starting that feed earlier in the day.

Easy weaning

Meals	What to eat	How to prepare	Tips
On waking up 7am–8am	Breast milk or formula milk	Lukewarm in the bottle	
Mid-morning 9.30am–10am	Fruit: cooked apple or pear, or raw banana	Pureed or mashed	Feed with a small baby spoon to accustom your child to this new way of being fed
Lunch 11.30am–12pm	Breast milk or formula milk	Lukewarm in the bottle	
Afternoon 3pm–4pm	Breast milk or formula milk	Lukewarm in the bottle	
Dinner 6.30pm–7pm	Breast milk or formula milk	Lukewarm in the bottle	The total amount of formula milk consumed within one day should be between 800 ml and 1 litre, depending on the weight of the baby

Feeding from 6 months onwards: baby's first taste of cereal

From the sixth month onwards, the weaning process speeds up slightly. After their first taste of solid food, cooked and pureed vegetables or fruit, baby's first cereal can then be introduced into the midday feed alongside breast milk or formula. Start with baby rice, which is coarsely ground rice flour, mixed with vegetable broth (stock) made from a single variety of cooked, pureed vegetable. After this has been accepted by the child, pureed vegetables, pureed fruit and, eventually, pureed meat can be gradually introduced into the mixture.

Vegetable broth and baby rice

After introducing cooked and pureed or fresh and raw fruit, and once your baby has come to accept the use of a spoon at feeding time, you can start to give them their first vegetable broth (stock), which will be the base for all the other cereals they are fed. Initially make the broth with either carrot, potato, or zucchini (courgette). The baby rice or cereal is then added to the broth. At this first stage this is made from rice flour, cornmeal, or tapioca flour because they don't contain gluten—a protein present in certain grains and their derivatives—which is best not to introduce too early. Added to these simple ingredients is olive oil, the most suitable vegetable fat, and a little grated hard cheese, such as Cheddar, Parmesan, or Pecorino.

New vegetables and finally meat

Other vegetables can then be gradually added, one at a time, to the broth (stock), such as fennel, celery, onion, and beet greens. Similarly, a little of these new vegetables can be pureed and added to the baby rice or cereal.

Eventually, meat can be introduced into your baby's diet. It's best to start with white meat, such as turkey and chicken, which is tender, lean, and more easily digested, before transitioning to red meat.

For those times you need to do so, such as when traveling, it is fine to use commercially available pureed meat bought in jars. Ready-made baby food products are easy to digest because they are well blended and also safe with regard to the source of their ingredients. The smooth consistency of these purees also makes them easier to swallow.

However, it is just as easy to save a slice of meat from your roast dinner and mince that into a puree yourself. That way you can control exactly what your baby is eating. Do remember not to season the meat when you are cooking the family meal as your baby's puree should not contain any added salt. Unless very well minced, meats pureed in the food processor at home may be less easy to digest because they contain air and is trickier for the gastric juices to break down.

New food discoveries

- vegetable broth (stock) made with: carrot, potato, zucchini (courgette), or pumpkin
- pureed vegetables: carrot, potato, zucchini (courgette), or pumpkin
- cereals: baby rice, cornmeal, and tapioca
- pureed meat: turkey, chicken, beef, and lamb
- cheese: grated hard cheese, such as Cheddar, Parmesan, or Pecorino
- condiments: extra virgin olive oil

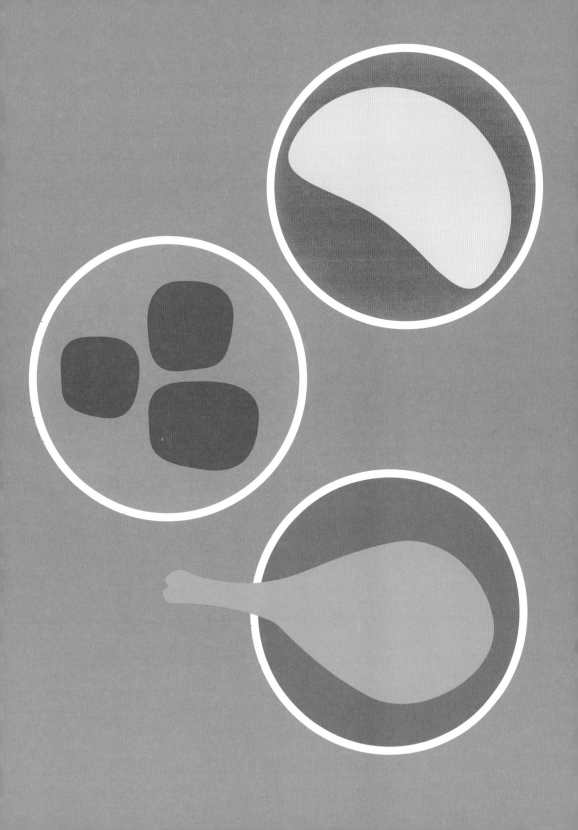

Feeding from 6 months onwards: cereals, vegetables, and meat

During this second stage of weaning, it is important not to worry if your infant seems to be eating a little less than the amount prescribed on weaning charts and in manuals. And it is even more important not to force your child to eat something they reject just because of its nutritional importance.

Regardless of the time taken and the effort made to prepare a cereal for your baby, if they do not open their mouth and instead turn away, never force them to eat. The correct thing to do is to give up on this particular attempt at feeding that food, but instead alternate different foods by color, flavor, and texture. When your baby refuses the food you are offering them, while it is wise to try again at the next mealtime, meanwhile you can give them a little of something that you know they will eat, such as pureed fruit.

Be patient and simply try again with the same food at the next meal or, if necessary, leave it for a day or two before trying again. You may like to try preparing the same ingredient in a slightly different way until your child accepts the new flavor.

Keep offering a variety of foods, even ones they do not seem to like. It may take multiple tries for your baby to get used to new foods, flavors, and textures. There will be days when they eat more, others when they eat less, and then days when they reject everything. This is normal. Eat together as a family whenever you can. Babies learn by copying.

Meals	What to eat	How to prepare	Tips
On waking up 7am–8am	Breast milk or formula milk	Lukewarm in the bottle	
Mid-morning 9.30am–10am (optional)	Fruit: cooked apple or pear, or raw banana	Pureed or mashed, with no added sugar	Feed with a small baby spoon, or dilute it with water and give in a bottle
Lunch 11.30am–12pm	Cereal with vegetables prepared with vegetable broth + baby rice, corn, or tapioca + extra virgin olive oil + grated hard cheese	The ingredients are pureed in a base of vegetable broth with no added salt. The cereal can be gradually enriched. By the end of the sixth month, mix with any of the new foods permitted at this age	Feed lukewarm with a small baby spoon in increasing amounts until the portion size recommended by your pediatrician is achieved
Afternoon 3pm–4pm	Breast milk or formula milk	Lukewarm in the bottle	
Dinner 6.30pm–7pm	Breast milk or formula milk	Lukewarm in the bottle	Alongside milk, offer cooled, boiled water to your baby throughout the day

Feeding from 7 months onwards: adding a second cereal meal

By the seventh month, four or five weeks after the midday cereal meal has first been introduced, it's time to replace your baby's evening milk or formula feed with a second meal of cereal. The range of cereals can now be expanded by experimenting with wheat, barley, and oats. The novelty now is the introduction of cereal with cheese.

Supplying protein and calcium

Like meat, cheese is a source of high biological value protein and calcium, which is essential for strengthening bones and the skeleton. You can start by using low-fat cheeses, such as cream cheese, or portions of low-fat processed cheese. It's also time for your child to gradually be introduced to other kinds of meat. Any kind of meat can be used at this age.

Pureed baby food

Pick up pots or sachets of purees to use when out and about, traveling, or too busy to cook fresh purees. They can be used up to the age of 24 months.

In regards to fruit, you can start using fresh seasonal fruit in grated form. Fruit juices generally contain added sugar but no fiber. It's best not to offer them in place of fresh fruit, either as a drink during meals or as an afternoon snack.

Avoid salt and sugar until after the second year

It's best not to add salt to cereal or any foods during the child's first and second years. This allows the infant to appreciate the natural flavor of each ingredient rather than become accustomed to salty foods. It's also not advisable to add sugar or other kinds of sweeteners to food, so that the infant doesn't get used to very sweet flavors.

New food discoveries

- in addition to any kind of pureed meat, you can also add small pieces of cooked ham and low-fat fresh cheeses, such as cream cheese, to the cereal
- you can now feed your baby any other seasonal fruit, such as plums, but take care to remove the stones or pips to avoid any choking hazards
- the range of vegetables can be expanded to include leek and fennel, but only use one of these at a time

Feeding from 7 months onwards: pasta and cheese

It is important to create a happy atmosphere during meals. However, mealtimes should be regularly scheduled, and great composure is needed in the face of eventual—and predictable—refusals of food.

Give lots of smiles, avoid raising your voice, issuing any threats, or adopting any kind of tricks. If your infant refuses to eat, it is counterproductive to cajole them with toys while trying to create the right moment to put food into their mouth. It is better to try again at the next meal without offering them any other food during the interval.

Meals	What to eat	How to prepare	Tips
On waking up 7am–8am	Breast milk or formula milk; baby breakfast cereal with fresh fruit	Lukewarm in the bottle	Offer your baby pre-boiled, cooled tap water to drink throughout the day
Mid-morning 9.30am–10am (optional)	Fruit: raw fresh apples, pears, bananas, and plums	Peeled, mashed, or pureed plum with no added sugar	Feed with a small baby spoon or diluted with pre-boiled, cooled tap water in the bottle
Lunch 11.30am–12pm	Cereal with meat prepared with vegetable or meat broth + different pureed vegetables + soup pasta, rice, or durum wheat semolina + extra virgin olive oil + pureed meat or cooked ham	Introduce new ingredients gradually, one at a time, blended with the vegetable or meat broth always made with fresh vegetables and with no added salt	Feed lukewarm with a small baby spoon in increasing amounts until the portion size recommended by your pediatrician is achieved, and with the addition of new ingredients every three or four days
Afternoon 3–4pm	Breast milk, formula milk or full-fat yogurt + fresh fruit + bread or toast		Feed with a small baby spoon, as for the lunchtime meal
Dinner 6.30pm–7pm	Cereal with cheese prepared like the lunchtime meal but with different cheeses such as Parmesan instead of meat	Introduce new cheeses gradually, one every three or four days	Feed with a small baby spoon, as for the lunchtime meal

Feeding from 8 months onwards:
a gradual education in taste

By their eighth month, babies will have already experienced many different flavors and will be ready for even more. Even in this second stage of food discovery, the rule is to introduce new tastes gradually and with patience. And the possibility of trying out many interesting ingredients makes the experience stimulating for baby.

Taste buds in action

Weaning is the moment when a child will come into contact with many new flavors for the first time. During this period, infants' taste buds are being activated to identify and appreciate each new food. By the sixth month, they're already able to communicate their preferences through the gusto-facial reflex linked by the stimuli produced by food. This can be seen in the expression of pleasure a baby makes after sampling something sweet, compared to the grimace of repulsion they make after tasting something sour or bitter. Towards the end of the first 12 months, a baby's perception of taste is clearly evident and highly personal, as well as being in part hereditary.

Hereditary food preferences

Any food happily eaten by an expectant mother during her pregnancy, such as garlic, for instance, also becomes familiar to the unborn baby through the filtering mechanism of the placenta. However, the inexplicable rejection of a sprinkling of grated cheese on cereal is often justified by the same aversion in one of the two parents. This suggests that the rejection of some foods and craving for others is often hereditary. Infants' taste buds in the first year of life are still immature and have to be educated. It's therefore beneficial to gently and gradually bring them into contact with the greatest possible range of flavors.

New food discoveries

- pulses: lentils, garbanzo beans (chickpeas), and beans
- bone-free, lean fish: hake, plaice, and cod
- cooked egg yolk: first just a teaspoon, then later a whole one
- tomatoes, green beans, and spinach
- soup pasta (small pasta shapes)
- meat
- citrus and other fruits

Feeding from 8 to 10 months: fish, egg, and pulses

From the eighth month onward, new essential ingredients can be introduced into baby's diet, such as fish, which is an excellent source of complete protein. It's advisable to start off with the leanest white fish, including hake, plaice, and cod. After 12 months, almost any type of fish can be fed to your child, but not seafood. Always check any fish you are going to serve to your baby with the utmost vigilance for small bones on which they could choke.

A source of protein and fiber with a relatively high biological value, pulses, such as peas, lentils, and beans, can also be alternated with animal protein. However, together with cows' milk, egg is often one of the main causes of food allergies. It should therefore be introduced with great care. After the eighth month, try adding egg yolk to dishes, but only a teaspoon in soup or cereal at first and making sure it is cooked through by the heat of the food, building up to a whole cooked egg yolk—instead of meat—once a week.

Introducing more solid foods

Babies don't need to have all their teeth before starting to eat solid food. Remember that babies develop at different rates, with some starting to chew earlier than others, but by the age of 10 months, some infants are able to chew using their gums and to soften food with saliva so it can be swallowed without trouble.

At this point, babies can gradually be introduced to more coarsely pureed vegetables, pasta in larger shapes, and ground meat, which will allow them to experience the pleasure of chewing food. They can also be given sugar-free teething biscuits (rusks), but starting with soluble ones that dissolve easily in the mouth. Use your judgement and never leave your baby alone with food at any time.

Stimulate the senses

As your baby's appreciation of color and texture develops, give them foods that will stimulate their senses as well as their appetite. Brightly colored finger foods, such as steamed carrot sticks are often a hit with babies. Or try adding cooked peas to mash, or small pieces of soft fruit to a fruit puree.

Meals	What to eat	How to prepare	Tips
On waking up 7am–8am	Breast milk or formula milk + baby breakfast cereal + fruit	Lukewarm in the bottle	Offer your baby pre-boiled, cooled tap water to drink throughout the day
Mid-morning 9.30am–10am (optional)	Fruit: seasonal fruit can be introduced, such as peach, apricot, and citrus	Peeled and cut into small pieces	Served on a small plate to be eaten with the hands
Lunch 11.30am–12pm	Cereal prepared with vegetable broth + vegetables + soup pasta or baby rice + meat or cooked ham, or bone-free fish, or pulses (beans or lentils)	The ingredients are coarsely pureed or minced. Some particularly soft foods can be served as small morsels	Feed lukewarm with a suitable size baby spoon in increasing amounts until the portion size recommended by your pediatrician is achieved. Only add a new ingredient every three or four days
Afternoon 3pm–4pm	Breast milk, formula milk, or full-fat yogurt + fresh fruit	Puree the fruit and mix it into the yogurt	
Dinner 6.30pm–7pm	Cereal prepared like the lunchtime meal + cheese, or pulses (beans or lentils), or cooked egg yolk (instead of meat) once a week	The cheese can be given in small pieces, while cooked egg yolk can be introduced a little at a time	

Easy weaning

Feeding from 11 to 12 months: meals become more "grown-up"

After the tenth month, breast milk or formula milk is only given for baby's breakfast. Other feeding times, such as the mid-morning and afternoon snacks, lunch, and dinner, start to resemble grown-up meals. Coarser, more solid consistencies have appeared in baby's diet. At this age, a baby starts to appreciate the routine around mealtimes, making them feel secure and part of the family, and so it is important to eat as many meals together as possible.

At the age of 12 months, babies can regularly be fed morsels of soft cheese, small pieces of vegetables like carrot, potato, and zucchini (courgette), or segments of soft fruit. As soon as they gain more experience, an infant can try small pieces of turkey, chicken, or bone-free fish, which don't need much chewing—these can be given on a small plate.

Also, you can now introduce ingredients that have a more intense flavor, such as a few finely chopped herbs, onion, garlic, and spices. These natural ingredients will encourage your child to enjoy a variety of tastes and show them that delicious flavors in food can be natural rather than artificial.

Increasing autonomy

Small children like being given the opportunity to eat on their own, perhaps with their hands, because it makes them feel grown up. Furthermore, it is beneficial for the development of their hand-eye co-ordination, dexterity, and overall healthy-eating habits.

Supervising and indulging

Parents must always supervise each meal in order to make sure that the child doesn't put too many pieces of food into their own mouth at the same time, which could be a choking hazard. Each mouthful must be properly chewed and then swallowed. Infants must never be given foods that cannot be ground down with their gums or can be choked on, like whole nuts. (Always give any nuts in the form of smooth nut butters.)

When serving any meat that may contain bones, and especially fish that often contains very small bones, always check carefully and remove any bones you find as they may present a choking hazard for an infant.

New food discoveries

· pasta
· small amount of lean cooked ham
· boneless fish in small pieces
· sugar-free teething biscuits (rusks) with egg and gluten

Feeding from 11 to 12 months: learning from others

During weaning, it's very important that a child learns how to eat in the early stages of their development. It's a period of a few months when infants come into contact with the world of flavors and get ready to taste and appreciate everything. Eating together as a family, with parents and also perhaps siblings, or with other children at childcare centers, is a crucial experience for learning by imitation and participation. Infants will mirror the behavior of grown ups and copy their actions.

Easy weaning

Meals	What to eat	How to prepare	Tips
On waking up 7am–8am	Formula milk + baby breakfast cereal + fruit	Lukewarm in the bottle	Offer your baby pre-boiled, cooled tap water to drink throughout the day
Mid-morning 09.30am–10am (optional)	Fruit: seasonal fresh fruit, except strawberries and cherries	Peeled and cut into small pieces	Served on a small plate to be eaten with hands
Lunch 11.30am–12pm	Pasta with tomato and grated cheese or with a simple sauce of ground meat, bone-free fish, or pulses (beans or lentils)	The ingredients can be less finely ground, and the pasta can come in slightly larger shapes than soup pasta; pulses are pureed	Feed lukewarm with a small baby spoon in increasing amounts until the portion size recommended by your pediatrician is achieved, and with the addition of new ingredients every three or four days
Afternoon 3.30pm–4pm	Milk or full-fat yogurt + fresh fruit + 2 or 3 breadsticks	Cut the fruit into pieces, or puree the fruit and mix it with the yogurt	Fruit and teething biscuits (rusks) can both be eaten with hands
Dinner 6.30pm–7pm	Cereal prepared as in the preceding months + cheese or pulses (beans or lentils) or cooked egg yolk once a week. The cheese can now be hard, such as Cheddar or Gouda	The cheese can be cut up into small pieces	Small pieces of bread can also be given

Recipes for 6 to 7 months

Grated fruit

preparation time: 5 minutes
cooking time: none
makes: one portion

· 1 eating apple, such as Golden Delicious, or
1 eating pear, such as Bartlett (Williams) or
Concorde, or 1 ripe banana

Wash the apple or pear well, then peel, core
and grate the fruit, preferably using a plastic
fruit grater. Alternatively, peel, chop, and cook
the fruit with a little water until soft, then mash
into a puree. Put into a bowl and feed to your
baby with a suitable size baby spoon.

When feeding banana to your child, peel the
fruit first, cut off the black end and mash
the flesh onto a plate with a fork. Do not add
any sugar or lemon juice, which can cause an
allergic reaction. Feed the fruit to your child
with a suitable size baby spoon.

Always choose ripe and healthy looking fruit.
Start with sweeter varieties of apple, such
as Golden Delicious, which is a fantastic
apple with a great balance of sweet and tart
flavors, before introducing other varieties,
such as Stark or Royal Gala later on. Avoid
sharp-tasting apples, such as Granny Smith,
especially at the beginning.

Yellow or red Bartlett (Williams) or Concorde
pears are preferable at first because they are
softer and juicier. Bosc pears are also suitable,
provided they are very ripe.

Equipment needed:
Vegetable peeler, paring knife, plastic fruit
grater, fork.

The first solid food:
Other than milk, baby rice, cooked and pureed
vegetables, or cooked and pureed fruit will be
the first food that your baby comes into contact
with. It is not meant to replace any bottle feeds,
but mainly serves the purpose of getting your
child used to being fed with a spoon.

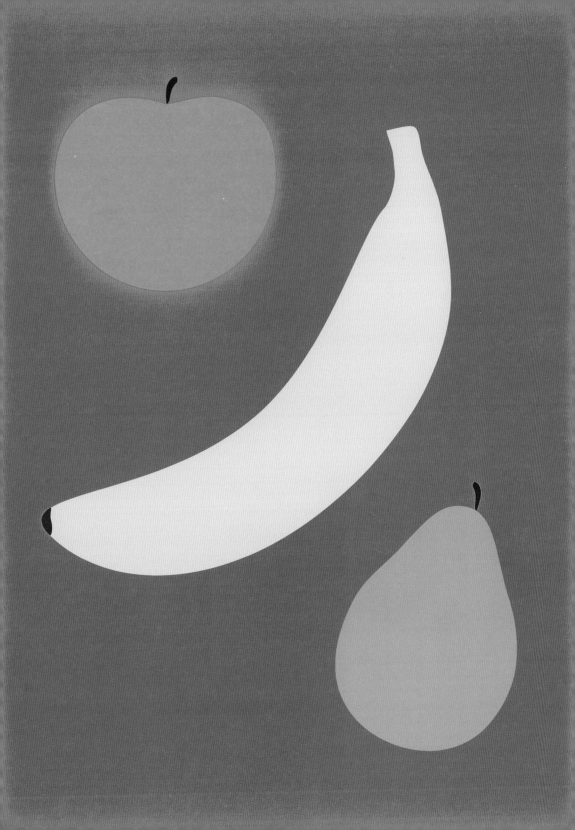

Vegetable broth

preparation time: 5 minutes
cooking time: 1 hour
makes: two or three (¾–1-cup/180–240-ml/
6–8-fl oz) portions

· 1 potato
· 1 carrot
· 1 zucchini (courgette)
· 4 cups/1 liter/34 fl oz water

Peel the potato. Peel and cut off both ends of the carrot. Cut off both ends of the zucchini (courgette). Slice all the vegetables into chunks.

Wash all the vegetables thoroughly and put into a pan. Add the water, partially cover the pan with the lid, and bring to a boil over high heat. Lower the heat and let simmer until the liquid is reduced by almost half, about 50 minutes. Do not add any salt or a bouillon (stock) cube.

Strain the broth (stock) into a jug and discard the cooked vegetable pieces. Measure out and use the required amount of vegetable broth as specified in the recipe you are following.

Store any remaining vegetable broth in the refrigerator for 24 hours, or divide it into individual portions and store in the freezer. To use, thaw the broth in the microwave for a few minutes or in a saucepan over low heat, but always check the heat of any food before feeding it to your baby.

Equipment needed:
Vegetable peeler, paring knife, saucepan with lid, fine-mesh strainer, measuring jug.

New vegetables:
Start by making a broth with potato, carrot, and zucchini. Once your baby has accepted this basic broth, you can gradually introduce other vegetables to the recipe. However, only introduce a new vegetable every four or five days, so that you can look out for any intolerances or allergic reactions. After potato, carrot, and zucchini, the next vegetables to bring in to a broth are sweet onion, leeks, pumpkin, artichoke hearts, green beans, celery, lettuce, cabbage, a few spinach leaves, or Swiss chard leaves.

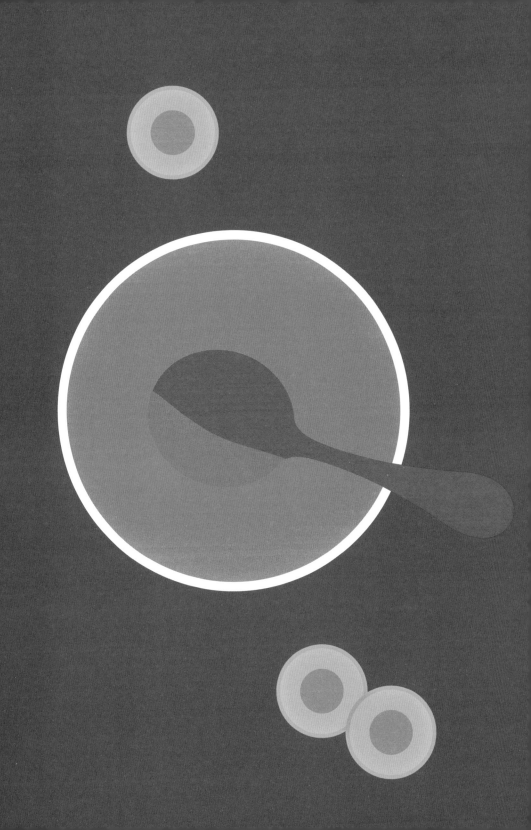

Baby's first cereal with rice

preparation time: 5 minutes
cooking time: 5 minutes
makes: one portion

· ⅔–¾ cup/150–180 ml/5–6 fl oz
  vegetable broth (stock) (see page 58)
· 3–4 level tbsp instant baby rice, cream
  of corn, ground tapioca, or ground millet
· 1 tsp extra virgin olive oil

Warm the vegetable broth in a pan and whisk in the instant cereal of your choice. Transfer to a small plate. Season with the olive oil, mix again, and serve. Do not add any salt.

Choose a good-quality, cold-pressed extra virgin olive oil. At first, use a mild oil and avoid any with strong or more pungent flavors.

This is a "transitional" cereal that should only be given for a few days, until the child gets used to the new taste. After three or four days, add vegetables, fruit, or meat to the cereal.

Equipment needed:
Saucepan, small stainless steel whisk.

Gluten-free cereals until seven months:
This solid meal should replace the second bottle of the day. Until the end of the sixth month, use only gluten-free cereals, such as baby rice, corn, tapioca, or millet, which can generally be found at health food stores.

Adjust the consistency of the cereal by varying the ratio of broth to cereal. It is better to start with a runnier mixture, adding more cereal for a thicker texture.

Your baby will not be able to eat a whole portion at first; they will probably manage only a few spoonfuls. If so, halve the suggested portion, supplemented with raw fruit, and refrigerate the rest for the next mealtime.

Baby's first cereal with lamb

preparation time: 5 minutes
cooking time: 5 minutes
makes: one portion

· ¾–1 cup/180–240 ml/6–8 fl oz vegetable broth (stock) (see page 58)
· 4–5 level tbsp instant baby rice, cream of corn, tapioca, or millet
· small slice of leftover cooked lamb
· 1 tsp extra virgin olive oil

Warm the vegetable broth (stock) in a pan and whisk in the instant cereal of your choice.

Blend the cooked meat in a food processor to a smooth puree. Add the pureed meat to the pan and mix well.

Transfer the cereal mixture to a small plate. Season with the olive oil, mix again, and serve. Do not add any salt.

Equipment needed:
Saucepan, small stainless steel whisk, food processor.

Meat for iron:
Meat replenishes the iron supplied to baby by the mother during pregnancy, which is practically used up by the fifth or sixth month. Start by introducing lamb into your baby's diet, which is the meat that produces the least allergic reaction. After seven or eight days, it is then possible to introduce turkey, chicken, and then beef in succession.

Leftover meat and vegetables:
When you roast lamb or other meats for your own dinner, avoid seasoning the meat so that you can feed some of the leftovers to your baby. Similarly, when you cook vegetables keep any leftovers for pureeing and adding to your baby's meals. Just make sure that when you cook vegetables, you do not add any salt to the water.

Baby's first cereal with meat and vegetables

preparation time: 10 minutes
cooking time: 10 minutes
makes: one portion

· ¾–1 cup/180–240 ml/6–8 fl oz vegetable
  broth (stock) (see page 58)
· 2 tbsp pureed vegetables, reserved from
  the vegetable broth
· 4–5 level tbsp instant baby rice, cream
  of corn, tapioca, or millet
· small slice of leftover cooked lamb or turkey
· 1 tsp extra virgin olive oil

After preparing and straining the vegetable broth (stock), do not discard the vegetable pieces. Using a hand-held immersion (stick) blender or food processor, puree the strained vegetables to a creamy consistency.

Warm the vegetable broth in a pan, add 2 tablespoons of the pureed vegetables and whisk in the instant cereal of your choice, whisking well to keep any lumps from forming.

Any leftover pureed vegetables can be divided into small portions and then frozen or stored in the refrigerator for up to 24 hours for subsequent meals.

Blend the cooked meat in a food processor to a smooth puree. Stir the pureed meat through the cereal, mixing well. Transfer the cereal mixture to a small plate. Season with the olive oil, mix again, and serve. Do not add any salt.

Equipment needed:
Hand-held immersion (stick) blender or food processor, saucepan, small stainless steel whisk.

Adjust according to appetite:
If your little one is very hungry, increase the amount of pureed vegetables you add to the cereal.

If your baby has a tendency to suffer from constipation, you should only add pureed zucchini (courgette) to the cereal. However, if they suffer from diarrhea, you can add pureed carrot and potato.

Millet porridge with potatoes, broccoli, and turkey

preparation time: 10 minutes
cooking time: 30 minutes
makes: one portion

· 1 potato
· 2 cups/500 ml/17 fl oz water
· 4 broccoli florets
· 4–5 level tbsp millet porridge
· small slice of leftover cooked turkey
· 1 tsp extra virgin olive oil

Peel and dice the potato. Put into a pan, cover with the water, partially cover with the lid, and bring to a boil over a high heat. Lower the heat and let simmer, about 15 minutes.

Wash the broccoli florets and cut the stalks into slices for quicker cooking. Add the broccoli to the pan with the potato. Continue to cook for a further 10 minutes, until the broccoli is tender.

Strain the vegetable broth (stock). Using a hand-held immersion (stick) blender or food processor, puree the strained vegetables. Warm ¾–1 cup/180–240 ml/6–8 fl oz of the broth in a pan and whisk in the instant cereal, whisking well to keep any lumps from forming.

Blend the cooked turkey in a food processor to a smooth puree. Stir 2 tablespoons of the pureed vegetables and the pureed meat through the cereal, mixing well. Transfer the cereal mixture to a small plate. Season with the olive oil, mix again, and serve. Do not add salt.

Any leftover pureed vegetables can be divided into small portions and then frozen or stored in the refrigerator for up to 24 hours for subsequent meals.

Equipment needed:
Vegetable peeler, paring knife, pan with lid, hand-held immersion (stick) blender or food processor, fine-mesh strainer, small stainless steel whisk.

Discovering other flavors:
Gradually introduce your baby to the flavor of broccoli, cabbage, or cauliflower by adding a few leaves or florets to the basic vegetable broth recipe (see page 58), pureeing them together with the other vegetables. Only make this cereal with broccoli once your baby is used to this flavor. Before concluding that your baby doesn't like a certain food, let them try it at least five or six times to get used to the flavor. You can only decide that it is really not for them after experimenting several times.

Recipes for 6 to 7 months

Rice, corn, and tapioca cereal with chicken and squash

preparation time: 5 minutes
cooking time: 30 minutes
makes: one portion

· 1 potato
· ¾ cup/100 g/3½ oz butternut or acorn squash
· 2½ cups/600 ml/20 fl oz water
· 4–5 tbsp instant baby rice, corn, or tapioca
· small slice of leftover cooked chicken
· 1 tsp extra virgin olive oil

Wash, peel, and cut the potato and squash into small dice. Put into a pan, cover with the water, partially cover with the lid and bring to a boil over a high heat. Lower the heat and let simmer, about 30 minutes.

Strain the vegetable broth (stock). Using a hand-held immersion (stick) blender or food processor, puree the strained vegetables.

Warm ¾–1 cup/180–240 ml/6–8 fl oz of the broth in a pan and whisk in the instant cereal, whisking well to keep any lumps from forming.

Blend the cooked chicken in a food processor to a smooth puree. Stir 2 tablespoons of the pureed vegetables and the pureed meat through the cereal, mixing well. Transfer the cereal mixture to a small plate. Season with the olive oil, mix again, and serve. Do not add salt.

Leftover pureed vegetables can be divided into portions and frozen or stored in the refrigerator for up to 24 hours for subsequent meals.

Equipment needed:
Vegetable peeler, paring knife, pan with lid, hand-held immersion (stick) blender or food processor, fine-mesh strainer, small stainless steel whisk.

Sweet and tasty squash:
Butternut squash is the optimal choice as it is super sweet and packed with vitamin A.

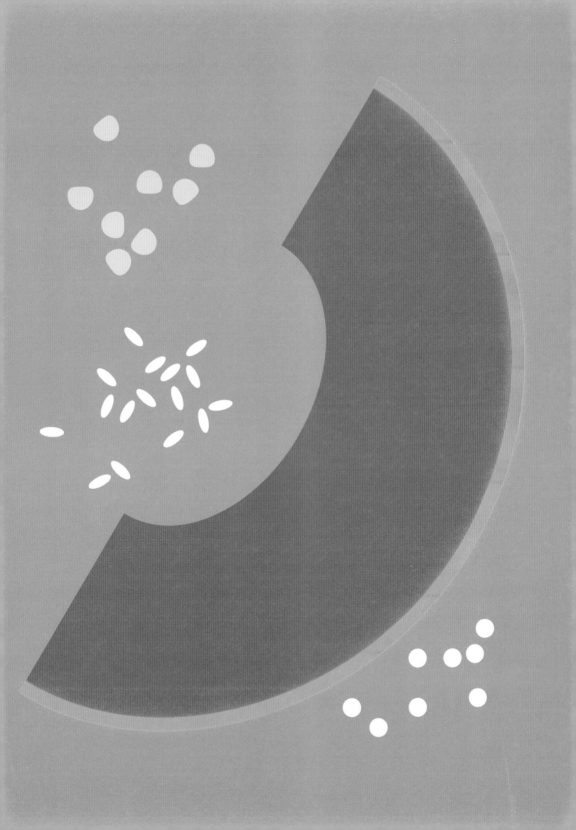

Baby rice with potato, artichokes, and lamb

preparation time: 15 minutes
cooking time: 40 minutes
makes: one portion

· 1 potato
· ¾-in/2-cm piece of leek, white only
· 2 artichokes
· 2½ cups/600 ml/20 fl oz water
· 4–5 tbsp instant baby rice
· small slice of leftover cooked lamb
· 1 tsp extra virgin olive oil

Wash, peel, and dice the potato. Wash the piece of leek thoroughly and halve. Wash the artichokes, remove the leaves and choke, leaving only the hearts, then rinse under running water. Put all the vegetables in a pan, cover with the water, partially cover with the lid, and bring to a boil over a high heat. Lower the heat and let simmer, about 30 minutes.

Strain the vegetable broth (stock). Using a hand-held immersion (stick) blender or food processor, puree the strained vegetables.

Warm ¾–1 cup/180–240 ml/6–8 fl oz of the vegetable broth in a pan and whisk in the rice, whisking well to keep any lumps from forming.

Blend the cooked lamb in a food processor to a smooth puree. Stir 2 tablespoons of the pureed vegetables and the pureed meat through the cereal, mixing well. Transfer the cereal mixture to a small plate. Season with the olive oil, mix again, and serve. Do not add salt.

Any leftover pureed vegetables can be divided into small portions and then frozen or stored in the refrigerator for up to 24 hours for subsequent meals.

Equipment needed:
Vegetable peeler, paring knife, pan with lid, hand-held immersion (stick) blender or food processor, fine-mesh strainer, small stainless steel whisk.

Keep experimenting, but gradually:
Your baby may not immediately like the flavor of leek. Before making this new cereal, try adding a little piece of leek to the basic vegetable broth recipe (see page 58) to get them used to the flavor. Do not be surprised if your child refuses food at some point, even if they are healthy and normally eat well—they may be teething. At such a time, even contact with the spoon can cause discomfort and make milk more appealing.

Evening cereal with cheese

preparation time: 5 minutes
cooking time: 5 minutes
makes: one portion

- ¾–1 cup/180–240 ml/6–8 fl oz vegetable broth (stock) (see page 58)
- 4–5 tbsp instant baby rice
- 2 tbsp pureed vegetables
- 1 tbsp grated hard cheese, such as Parmesan
- 1 tsp extra virgin olive oil

Warm the vegetable broth in a pan. Whisk in the instant baby rice, whisking well to keep lumps from forming. Stir in the pureed vegetables, mixing well. Transfer the cereal mixture to a small plate. Add the grated cheese and the olive oil, mix again, and serve. Do not add any salt.

Besides the hard cheese, you can gradually introduce fresh, pasteurized cream cheeses, such as ricotta, Philadelphia, and Petit-Suisse, one at a time. Use ⅛ cup/30 g/1 oz fresh or cream cheese to make one portion of cereal.

Equipment needed:
Saucepan, small stainless steel whisk, grater.

Other novelties:
Cereal with cheese can be incorporated into the meal plan for baby at seven months. Serve it in the evening as the second main meal of the day. About a month after you start feeding your baby solid food, you can then introduce it at lunchtime. Once cheese has been introduced into the diet, you can feed cereal with meat and vegetables for lunch and then with cheese and vegetables for dinner.

Millet porridge with zucchini, ricotta, and grated cheese

preparation time: 5 minutes
cooking time: 20 minutes
makes: one portion

· 1 zucchini (courgette)
· ⅛ cup/20 g/¾ oz sweet onion
· a few thyme leaves
· 1⅔ cups/400 ml/13½ fl oz water
· 5 tbsp millet porridge
· 1 tsp grated hard cheese, such as Parmesan
· 1 tbsp ricotta cheese
· 1 tsp extra virgin olive oil

Peel the zucchini (courgette) and the onion. Wash all the vegetables and herbs thoroughly, then halve the zucchini and slice the onion and put into a pan. Add the water, which should cover the vegetables, partially cover with the lid, and bring to a boil over a high heat. Lower the heat and let simmer, about 20 minutes.

Strain the vegetable broth (stock) into a jug. Using a hand-held immersion (stick) blender or food processor, puree the zucchini and onion and set aside.

Pour ¾ cup/180 ml/6 fl oz of the strained broth into the pan and add the pureed zucchini and onion. Place the pan over the heat. Whisk in the cream of millet until dissolved.

Remove from the heat, add both the cheeses and mix well to a creamy consistency. Transfer the cereal mixture to a small plate. Season with the olive oil, mix again, and serve. Do not add any salt.

Equipment needed:
Vegetable peeler, paring knife, saucepan with lid, fine-mesh strainer, small stainless steel whisk, hand-held immersion (stick) blender or food processor, small stainless steel whisk.

Remedy for sluggish digestion:
Infants find this cereal particularly appealing. Happily, because it contains zucchini, it is particularly suitable for babies who suffer from sluggish digestion or constipation.

Baby rice with fennel and cream cheese

preparation time: 5 minutes
cooking time: 40 minutes
makes: one portion

· 1 small potato
· 2 fennel hearts
· a few celery leaves
· 1⅔ cups/400 ml/13½ fl oz water
· 4–5 tbsp instant baby rice
· ⅛ cup/30 g/1 oz pasteurized soft cream
  cheese, such as ricotta, Philadelphia,
  or Petit-Suisse
· 1 tsp extra virgin olive oil

Peel the potato. Cut the fennel hearts into quarters and remove the outer layers.

Wash all the vegetables and celery leaves thoroughly and put into a pan. Add the water, partially cover with the lid, and bring to a boil over a high heat. Lower the heat and let simmer, about 30 minutes.

Strain the vegetable broth (stock) into a jug. Using a hand-held immersion (stick) blender or food processor, puree the strained potato and fennel and set aside.

Heat ¾–1 cup/180–240 ml/6–8 fl oz of the strained vegetable broth in the pan with 2 tablespoons of the pureed potato and fennel. Whisk in the baby rice until dissolved. Remove from the heat, add the cheese, and mix well to a creamy consistency. Transfer the cereal mixture to a small plate. Season with the olive oil, mix again, and serve. Do not add any salt.

Any leftover pureed vegetables can be divided into small portions and then frozen or stored in the refrigerator for up to 24 hours for subsequent meals.

Equipment needed:
Vegetable peeler, paring knife, saucepan with lid, fine-mesh strainer, hand-held immersion (stick) blender or food processor, measuring jug, stainless steel whisk.

Tender hearts with fewer fibers:
Only use fennel hearts, as they are more tender and less fibrous. The sweet flavor of this vegetable is generally appealing to babies. However, from time to time, when the little one is feeling very tired, they may have no desire to eat a dish that they normally enjoy. Do not worry. At these moments, a good feed of milk and cereal is a valid and welcome replacement.

Baby's first dessert with fruit

preparation time: 5 minutes
cooking time: none
makes: one portion

· ½ eating apple, such as Golden Delicious
· ½ eating pear, such as Bartlett (Williams)
· 2 sugar-free teething biscuits (rusks)
· ½ cup/100 ml/3½ fl oz breast milk or made-up
  formula milk

Wash, peel, and core the apple and pear. Combine the apple, pear, teething biscuits (rusks), and breast milk or formula milk in a blender or food processor and blend for a few seconds until smooth. Transfer the mixture to a small plate and serve with a suitable size baby spoon.

The leftover apple and pear halves can be whizzed up in a blender with a little apple or orange juice to make a quick drink for any older members of the family.

Equipment needed:
Vegetable peeler, paring knife, blender or food processor.

Also in the bottle:
This is actually more of a snack than a dessert, and does not replace any meals. It can be given mid-morning, if your baby has their first meal very early, or mid-afternoon. In this case, you can increase the amount of milk and either give it to your baby in the bottle or before the usual bottle feed.

Recipes for 8 to 24 months

Chicken or beef broth

preparation time: 5 minutes
cooking time: 40 minutes
makes: two or three (1-cup/240-ml/8-fl oz)
portions

· 3 cups/1 kg/2 lb 4 oz skinless chicken or
  lean beef
· 8 cups/2 liters/70 fl oz water
· 1 potato
· 1 small onion
· 1 carrot
· 1 celery stalk with leaves

Put the meat of your choice in a pan, cover with the water, and bring to a boil over a high heat. Using a slotted spoon, skim off any scum that floats to the surface. Repeat this several times.

Peel the potato and the onion. Peel and cut off both ends of the carrot. Cut off both ends of the celery stalk.

Wash all the vegetables thoroughly. Add the vegetables to the pan with the meat, partially cover with the lid, and simmer over a medium heat for 40 minutes for chicken and 2 hours for beef. Do not add any salt or a bouillon (stock) cube.

Let the broth (stock) cool, then filter through a strainer lined with cheesecloth to remove any fat and impurities. Discard the cooked vegetable pieces.

Measure out the required amount of broth as specified in the recipe you are following.

Store any remaining broth in the refrigerator for 24 hours, or divide it into 1-cup/240-ml/ 8-fl oz portions and store in individual containers in the freezer. To use, thaw the broth in the microwave for a few minutes or in a saucepan over low heat, but always check the heat of any food before feeding it to your baby.

Equipment needed:
Vegetable peeler, paring knife, saucepan with lid, fine-mesh strainer, cheesecloth, measuring jug.

The right cuts:
After nine months, meat broth can be used instead of vegetable broth. Start with chicken broth, before moving on to beef broth, which is more substantial. When making chicken broth, use the thigh or breast, and remove the skin so that there is less fat in the broth. The most suitable beef cuts are brisket and foreshank.

Baby's first "risi e bisi", or risotto with peas

preparation time: 5 minutes
cooking time: 35 minutes
makes: one portion

· 2 heaped tbsp fresh shelled peas
  or frozen petit pois
· ¾-in/2-cm piece of scallion (spring onion),
  white only
· ¼ cup/30 g/1 oz diced, lean, cooked ham
· 1 cup/240 ml/8 fl oz vegetable broth (stock)
  (see page 58)
· 2 tbsp baby rice
· 1 tsp extra virgin olive oil

Carefully rinse the peas, if using fresh. Wash and slice the scallion (spring onion). Place the vegetables in a pan and cover with water. Bring to a boil over a high heat and cook for 20–25 minutes. Strain the cooked vegetables and, using a hand-held immersion (stick) blender or a food processor, blend to a puree. Grind up the ham in a food processor.

Warm the vegetable broth (stock) in a pan. As it comes to the boil, add the baby rice and cook for 6–8 minutes, stirring continuously with a wooden spoon as if making risotto.

About 1 minute before the end of the cooking time, stir the pureed vegetables through the "risotto". Remove the pan from the heat and add the ham. Transfer the risotto to a small plate. Season with the olive oil, and serve. Do not add any salt.

Equipment needed:
Paring knife, pan, fine-mesh strainer, hand-held immersion (stick) blender or food processor, wooden spoon.

Cooked ham:
From the eighth month onward, you can add cooked ham to this risotto, an ingredient that goes well with peas. Choose a natural, phosphate-free product. Remove any fat and only use the lean parts.

Radicchio risotto:
When your baby reaches 12 months, try introducing radicchio cooked in a risotto. Soften a diced onion in some oil, then finely shred a few radicchio leaves and add them to the pan. Sauté the vegetables for 5 minutes and then add the baby rice and cook as usual.

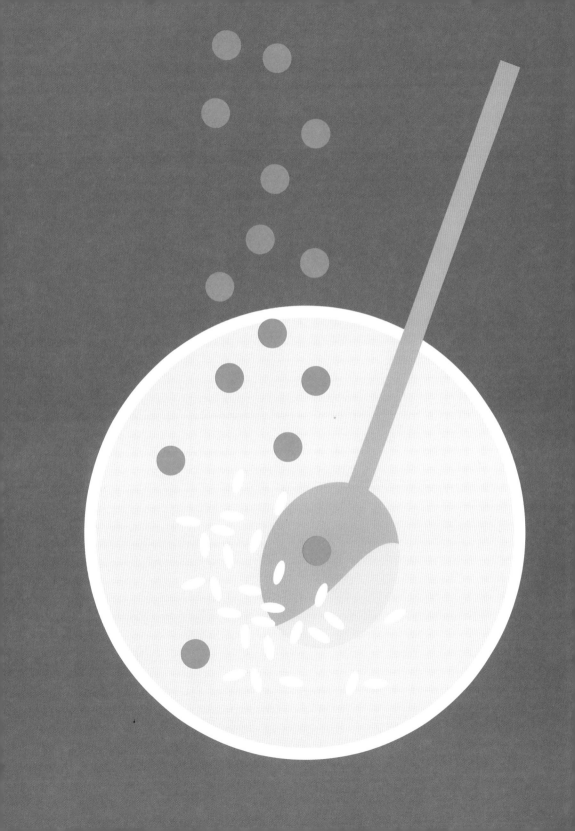

Risotto with tomato, green beans, and cream cheese

preparation time: 10 minutes
cooking time: 20 minutes
makes: one portion

· 1 handful fresh green beans
· 1 ripe tomato
· 1 cup/240 ml/8 fl oz vegetable broth (stock)
  (see page 58)
· 2 tbsp instant baby rice
· ⅛ cup/30 g/1 oz pasteurized soft cream
  cheese, such Philadelphia or Petit-Suisse
· 1 tsp extra virgin olive oil

Trim the ends off the beans, wash them well and cut into pieces. Bring a pan of water to the boil, plunge in the sliced beans and cook for 10–12 minutes. Drain the beans and, using a hand-held immersion (stick) blender or food processor, blend to a puree.

Wash the tomato and score the base with a cross. Blanch in boiling water for about 30 seconds, then drain, peel, and cut into quarters. Scoop out the seeds and mince the flesh.

Warm the vegetable broth (stock) in a pan and add the minced tomato. As it comes to the boil, add the baby rice and cook for 6–8 minutes, stirring continuously as if making risotto.

Stir the pureed beans through the "risotto" about 1 minute before the end of the cooking time. Remove the pan from the heat. Add the cheese to the pan, and stir until melted. Transfer to a small plate. Season with the olive oil, and serve. Do not add any salt.

Equipment needed:
Paring knife, saucepan, hand-held immersion (stick) blender or food processor, fine-mesh strainer, wooden spoon.

Sometimes the problem is consistency: Babies' preferences can be very subjective in terms of both the flavor and consistency of food. Regardless of whether or not they are teething, some babies only like their food "smooth", while others prefer to feel the "texture" of the ingredients. If your baby tends to reject any food with too many chunks or is only lightly pureed, you can further reduce it to a cream in a food processor. This trick is sometimes all it takes for a little one suddenly to appreciate a food they previously refused to eat—not because the problem was the flavor, but the consistency.

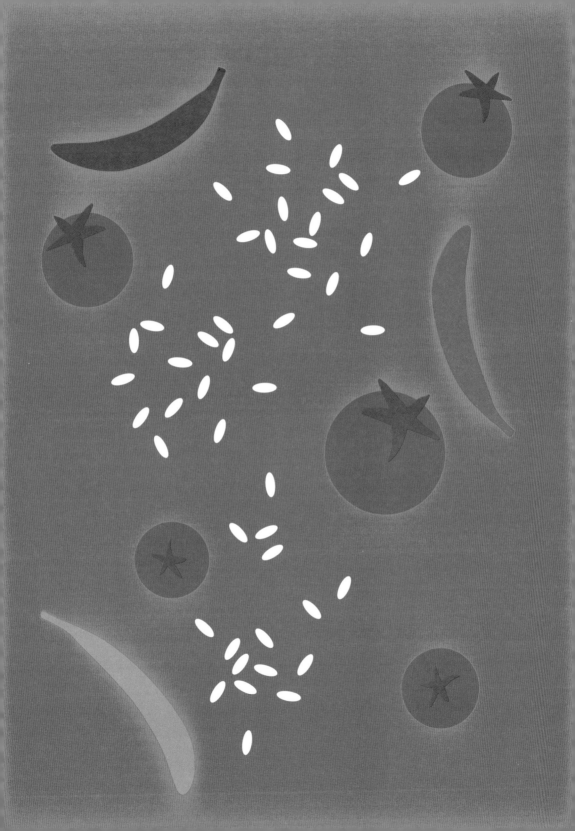

Fish broth

preparation time: 15 minutes
cooking time: 35 minutes
makes: about 4 cups/1 liter/34 fl oz

· 1 lb 2 oz/500 g mixed fish heads and bones
· 1 yellow onion
· 1 carrot
· 1 celery stalk
· 4 parsley sprigs
· 2 thyme sprigs
· 1 bay leaf
· 4 peppercorns
· 8 cups/2 liters/70 fl oz water

Rinse the fish heads and bones under cold running water to remove any traces of blood. Cut off the gills and discard. Peel the onion. Peel and cut off both ends of the carrot. Cut off both ends of the celery stalk.

Wash all the vegetables and herbs thoroughly and slice into small pieces. Put the vegetables in a pan with the cleaned fish heads and bones, herbs, peppercorns, and the water, partially cover with the lid and simmer over a medium heat for 35 minutes. Do not add any salt or a bouillon (stock) cube.

Let the broth (stock) cool, then filter through a strainer lined with cheesecloth to remove any impurities. Discard the cooked vegetable pieces.

Measure out the required amount of broth as specified in the recipe you are following.

Store any remaining broth in the refrigerator for up to two days, or divide it into 1 cup/ 240-ml/8-fl oz portions and store in individual containers in the freezer. To use, thaw the broth in the microwave for a few minutes or in a saucepan over low heat.

Equipment needed:
Vegetable peeler, paring knife, saucepan with lid, fine-mesh strainer, cheesecloth, measuring jug.

A mixture of flavors:
The heads and bones of gurnard and scorpion fish make a tasty broth, but sole, salmon, mullet, and trout carcasses also work well. Unless you have a family history of food allergies, you can add the shells of shrimp (prawns) and langoustines. If you're concerned about potential allergies, consult your pediatrician. When straining the broth, press well on the shells in the strainer to add more flavor to the broth. Make sure no pieces of shell or bones remain in any liquid you feed to your baby.

Recipes for 8 to 24 months

First cereal with fish

preparation time: 5 minutes
cooking time: 5 minutes
makes: one portion

· ½ plaice fillet, cleaned and skinned
· 1 cup/240 ml/8 fl oz vegetable or fish
  broth (stock) (see page 58 or 88)
· 2 tbsp pureed vegetables (potato, carrot,
  and zucchini/courgette)
· 4–5 level tbsp instant baby rice
· 1 tsp extra virgin olive oil

Carefully check the fish for bones and remove any found using tweezers.

Warm the broth (stock) in a saucepan, add the ½ plaice fillet and poach for 10 minutes or until cooked. Using a slotted spoon, remove the fish from the pan. Using a hand-held immersion (stick) blender or food processor, puree the fish until smooth.

Add the pureed vegetables to the broth, and whisk in the baby rice, whisking well to keep from forming lumps. Stir through the fish puree.

Transfer to a small plate. Season with the oil, mix again, and serve. Do not add any salt.

Equipment needed:
Tweezers, saucepan, slotted spoon, hand-held immersion (stick) blender or food processor, small stainless steel whisk.

You can freeze the remaining ½ plaice fillet for a future meal, or you can cook the whole plaice and either keep the cooked half in the refrigerator for 2 days or eat it yourself with some steamed vegetables for a healthy meal.

Cream of cereals with pumpkin, carrot, and sea bream

preparation time: 15 minutes
cooking time: 35 minutes
makes: one portion

· 1 small carrot
· 1 shallot
· ¼ cup/40 g/1½ oz diced pumpkin or butternut
  squash flesh
· 2½ cups/600 ml/20 fl oz water
· ¼ cup/50 g/1¼ oz white fish fillet, such as cod,
  haddock, sea bream, cleaned and skinless
· 4–5 tbsp instant baby rice or multigrain
  cereal powder
· 1 tsp extra virgin olive oil

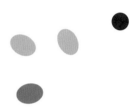

Peel the carrot and shallot, trim the ends, and cut into small chunks.

Wash the vegetables thoroughly and put into a pan with the water. Partially cover the pan with the lid and bring to a boil. Lower the heat and let simmer for 25–30 minutes. Strain the broth (stock) and set aside.

Meanwhile, wash the fish fillet and remove any bones with tweezers. Steam the fish for 5 minutes. Using a food processor, puree the steamed fish with the cooked vegetables.

Warm 1 cup/240 ml/8 fl oz of the vegetable broth in a pan, add the baby rice or cereal and whisk to stop from forming any lumps. Stir through the pureed fish and vegetables.

Transfer to a small plate. Season with the oil and serve. Do not add any salt.

Equipment needed:
Vegetable peeler, paring knife, pan with lid, fine-mesh strainer, tweezers, steamer basket, saucepan, small stainless steel whisk.

Watch out for bones:
Before cooking any fish, remove all the bones. Pass a finger over the fillet and if you feel a bone, remove it using tweezers. Take great care that all bones have been removed from any fish served to your baby.

Batch cooking:
To save any food waste, you can cook the whole squash. Peel the squash, remove the seeds, chop the flesh into small chunks, and boil in a pan of water until tender. Drain and puree the cooked vegetable, then spoon into ice cube trays and freeze.

Ligurian-style cream soup with potato, green beans, and plaice

preparation time: 5 minutes
cooking time: 35 minutes
makes: one portion

· 1 small potato
· 1 sweet onion
· 1 handful green beans
· a few basil leaves
· 1¾-oz/50-g plaice fillet, cleaned and skinned
· 4–5 tbsp instant baby rice or multigrain cereal powder
· 1 tsp extra virgin olive oil

Peel and cut the potato and onion into small chunks. Trim the ends of the beans and cut them in half. Wash all the vegetables and basil leaves thoroughly, put into a pan, and cover with 2 cups/500 ml/17 fl oz water. Bring to the boil, partially cover with the lid, and cook over a medium heat for 20 minutes. Do not add any salt or a bouillon (stock) cube.

Meanwhile, wash the fish fillet thoroughly, check for any bones, and steam for 5 minutes. Strain the broth (stock) from the cooked vegetables and set aside. Using a hand-held immersion (stick) blender or food processor, blend the cooked fish and vegetables to a puree.

Warm 1 cup/240 ml/8 fl oz of the reserved broth in a pan. Add the baby rice or multigrain cereal powder, whisking to stop lumps from forming. Stir through the pureed fish and vegetables.

Remove the pan from the heat. Transfer to a small plate, season with olive oil, and serve. Do not add any salt.

Store any remaining broth in the refrigerator for up to two days, or divide it into 1-cup/ 240-ml/8-fl oz portions and store in individual containers in the freezer. To use, thaw the broth in the microwave for a few minutes or in a saucepan over low heat.

Equipment needed:
Vegetable peeler, paring knife, pan with lid, saucepan, fine-mesh strainer, steamer basket, hand-held immersion (stick) blender or food processor, small stainless steel whisk.

Introducing fish:
You can start to introduce steamed, poached, or roasted fish into your baby's daily meals. However, you must be certain that the fish is fresh and all the bones have been removed first. Try sole, plaice, trout, hake, cod, snapper, sea bream, and sea bass. Avoid experimenting with shellfish until your child is at least 12 months old to reduce any risk of food poisoning or allergic reactions. Be vigilant, look for reactions and be ready to seek medical help, if necessary.

Oat or millet porridge with spinach, Swiss chard, and hake

preparation time: 15 minutes
cooking time: 25 minutes
makes: one portion

· ⅛ cup/30 g/1 oz baby spinach
· ⅛ cup/30 g/1 oz tender Swiss chard leaves
· 4 cups/1 liter/34 fl oz water
· ½ hake fillet, cleaned and skinned
· 4–5 tbsp finely ground baby oats or instant millet porridge
· 1 tsp extra virgin olive oil

Wash the baby spinach and Swiss chard leaves repeatedly under running water until there are no traces of soil left.

Bring the water to the boil in a pan, add the ½ hake fillet, and cook for 10 minutes. Using a slotted spoon, remove the fish from the pan and then add the baby spinach and Swiss chard to the boiling water.

Cook the greens for 5 minutes. Strain the broth (stock) from the cooked greens and set aside. Using your hands, squeeze the spinach and Swiss chard well to remove as much water as possible. Using a food processor, blend the cooked fish and greens to a puree.

Bring the broth (stock) to a boil in a saucepan. Add the baby oats or cream of millet, whisking well to keep from forming lumps. Stir through the pureed fish and vegetables. Transfer to a small plate. Season with the olive oil and serve. Do not add any salt.

Equipment needed:
Pan with lid, fine-mesh strainer, food processor, saucepan, small stainless steel whisk.

Fresh, seasonal vegetables:
If possible, use fresh vegetables that are in season. Baby spinach and Swiss chard are spring vegetables, although they can be found in stores practically throughout the year. You can also find bags of cleaned and washed spinach, baby spinach, and Swiss chard leaves packed in a modified atmosphere. If you use any of these, wash them carefully before cooking. When needed, you can cook a couple of cubes of frozen spinach and/or Swiss chard. Alternatively, replace the Swiss chard leaves with the same quantity of cabbage leaves.

You can freeze the remaining ½ hake fillet for a future meal, or you can cook the whole hake and either keep the cooked half in the refrigerator for two days or eat it yourself with some steamed vegetables for a healthy meal.

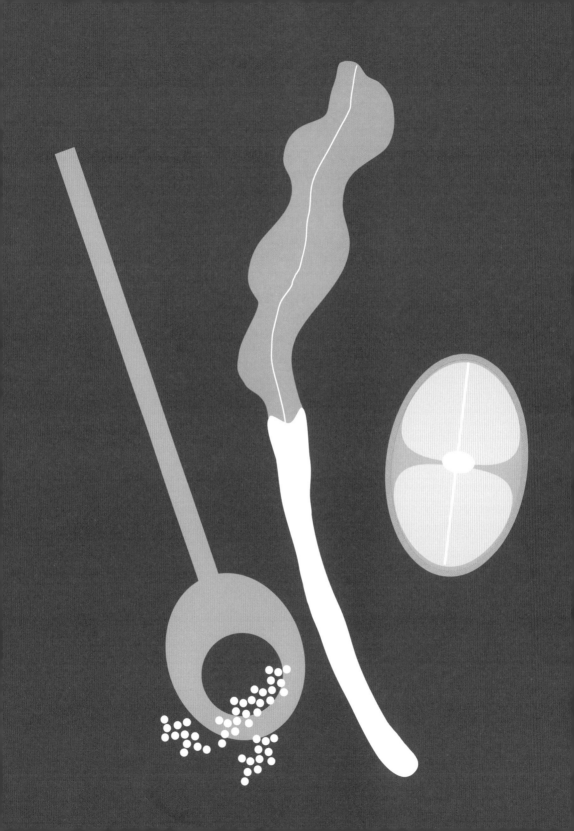

Pumpkin, leek, and sole risotto

preparation time: 15 minutes
cooking time: 40 minutes
makes: one portion

- ¼ cup/40 g/1½ oz leek, white part only
- ¼ cup/40 g/1½ oz diced pumpkin or
  butternut squash flesh
- ¼ cup/50 g/1¾ oz sole fillet, cleaned and
  skinned
- 1 cup/240 ml/8 fl oz vegetable or fish broth
  (stock) (see pages 58 or 88)
- 2 tbsp instant baby rice or multigrain
  cereal powder
- 1 tsp extra virgin olive oil

Wash and cut the leek into rounds. Put the
vegetables into a pan and cover with water.
Partially cover with the lid, and cook for
30 minutes. Drain.

Wash the fish fillet thoroughly and carefully
remove any bones using tweezers. Steam the
fish fillet for 5 minutes. Using a hand-held
immersion (stick) blender or food processor,
blend the fish with the cooked vegetables
to a puree.

Bring the broth (stock) to the boil in a pan. Add
the baby rice or cereal powder and cook for
2–3 minutes, stirring continuously. Stir through
the pureed fish and vegetables 30 seconds
before the end of the cooking time.

Remove the pan from the heat. Transfer to a
small plate, season with the olive oil, and serve.
Do not add salt.

Equipment needed:
Paring knife, pan with lid, fine-mesh strainer,
steamer basket, hand-held immersion
(stick) blender or food processor, saucepan,
wooden spoon.

Instant baby rice for less-developed babies:
Baby rice is a good first food for weaning as
it is gentle on a baby's immature digestive
system. Baby rice comes as a dry powder that
can be mixed with either formula or expressed
breast milk to the required consistency, which
is then served warm or at room temperature.
It is neutral in flavor, which means it can be
added to many different foods and mixed with
the amount of liquid needed to make the
desired consistency.

Creamy garbanzo bean and tomato soup

preparation time: 15 minutes
cooking time: 2 hours
makes: four portions

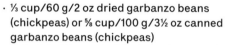

- ⅓ cup/60 g/2 oz dried garbanzo beans (chickpeas) or ⅝ cup/100 g/3½ oz canned garbanzo beans (chickpeas)
- 1 pinch baking soda (if using dried beans)
- 1 small rosemary sprig
- 2 ripe vine tomatoes
- 1 tsp extra virgin olive oil
- 1 tsp grated hard cheese, such as Parmesan

If using dried garbanzo beans (chickpeas), soak them in water with the baking soda for 12 hours. Drain the beans, rinse under running water, and put into a pan (preferably earthenware) with the rosemary, and cover with 2 in (5 cm) of water. Bring to the boil and simmer over a low heat, for about 1 hour. If using canned garbanzo beans, there is no need to soak or pre-cook them.

Score the base of each tomato with a cross, and blanch in boiling water for 30 seconds. Drain, peel, cut into quarters, and scoop out the seeds.

Add the tomato pieces to the pan with the beans and cook for a few minutes. If using canned beans, put them in a pan with a little vegetable broth, add the rosemary and tomato pieces, and cook for 5 minutes.

Strain the broth (stock) and set aside. Discard the rosemary. Using a hand-held immersion (stick) blender or food processor, puree the beans and tomatoes. Loosen with a little broth.

Divide the soup into four portions. Season the portion to be served immediately with the oil and grated cheese. Do not add salt.

Store the remaining portions in the refrigerator for up to 24 hours or in the freezer.

Equipment needed:
Pan (preferably earthenware), saucepan, paring knife, hand-held immersion (stick) blender or food processor, fine-mesh strainer.

Dried or canned pulses from the ninth month: After the ninth month, dried or canned pulses can be introduced into an infant's diet. If using canned, there is no need to soak or cook the pulses, just make sure you rinse them thoroughly before using. If using dried, soak overnight first. Cooking times for dried pulses can vary, but usually 1 hour is long enough. If you need a quicker option, the cooking time can be cut in half by using a pressure cooker.

Recipes for 8 to 24 months

Cream of cereals with ricotta, spinach, and cheese

preparation time: 15 minutes
cooking time: 10 minutes
makes: one portion

· ¼ cup/55 g/2 oz baby spinach
· 1 tbsp ricotta cheese
· 1 cup/240 ml/8 fl oz vegetable broth (stock)
· 4–5 tbsp instant baby rice, multigrain cereal
  powder, or cereal of your choice
· 1 tsp grated hard cheese, such as Parmesan
· 1 tsp extra virgin olive oil

Clean the spinach, removing any roots and harder stems. Wash repeatedly under running water until no traces of soil are left.

Bring 4 cups/1 liter/34 fl oz of water to the boil in a pan, add the spinach, and cook for 2–3 minutes. Drain and then squeeze well with your hands to remove any moisture. Using a hand-held immersion (stick) blender or food processor, puree the spinach together with the ricotta.

Bring the broth (stock) to the boil in a pan. Add the baby rice or cereal powder, whisking well to keep from forming lumps. Stir through the pureed spinach and ricotta.

Remove the pan from the heat. Transfer to a small plate. Season with the grated cheese and olive oil, mix, and serve. Do not add any salt.

Equipment needed:
Paring knife, pan, fine-mesh strainer, hand-held immersion (stick) blender or food processor, saucepan, small stainless steel whisk, grater.

Frozen vegetables only out of season:
The general rule is to use seasonal produce (see pages 160–191 for suggestions). If it is spring, for instance, use fresh spinach, preferably baby spinach with small and tender leaves. When out of season, use frozen spinach as an alternative. The frozen spinach that comes in cubes is very convenient because it lets you use the amount you require without having to thaw the entire packet. Simply put a cube into boiling water and cook for 5 minutes.

Creamy pea, lettuce, leek, and cream cheese soup

preparation time: 5 minutes
cooking time: 30 minutes
makes: one portion

· 1 cherry-sized piece of potato, peeled
· ½-in/1-cm length leek, white part only
· 2 lettuce leaves
· 1 tbsp fresh shelled peas or frozen petit pois
· 2 tbsp baby rice or cereal of your choice
· 1½ tbsp cream cheese
· 1 tsp extra virgin olive oil

Wash the potato, leek, lettuce, and peas, if using fresh. Bring 4 cups/1 liter/34 fl oz of water to the boil in a pan, add the potato and leek, partially cover with the lid, and cook for 10 minutes. Add the lettuce leaves and peas and cook for a further 10 minutes.

Strain the broth (stock) from the cooked vegetables and set aside. Using a hand-held immersion (stick) blender or food processor, blend the cooked vegetables to a puree.

Warm the broth in a pan and add the pureed vegetables. Add the baby rice or cereal powder, and cheese, mixing well with a whisk to keep from forming lumps.

Remove the pan from the heat. Transfer to a deep bowl or soup plate. Season with the olive oil, mix again, and serve. Do not add salt.

Equipment needed:
Paring knife, pan with lid, fine-mesh strainer, hand-held immersion (stick) blender or food processor, small stainless steel whisk.

Yes or no to hands in food?:
Most pediatric research suggests that babies should be allowed to touch what they are eating, so that they become familiar with food. The World Health Organization, the European Union, and the Department of Health all recommend giving your baby well-mashed or pureed foods at the beginning of weaning, as well as finger foods. A combination of weaning and baby-led weaning is ideal, however, to stop them from getting too messy, it may be enough to let the child hold a spoon of their own while being fed.

Creamy broccoli, Swiss chard, and zucchini soup with egg yolk

preparation time: 10 minutes
cooking time: 20 minutes
makes: one portion

· 1 walnut-sized baby broccoli floret
· 5 Swiss chard leaves
· ½ zucchini (courgette)
· 1 cup/240 ml/8 fl oz vegetable broth (stock) (see page 58)
· 2 tbsp instant baby rice or multigrain cereal powder
· 1 egg yolk
· 1 tsp extra virgin olive oil

Wash the vegetables thoroughly. Cut the broccolini stem into ¼-in/5-mm slices. Cut the zucchini (courgette) into equal rounds. Bring 2 cups/500 ml/17 fl oz water to the boil in a pan, add the broccolini, zucchini pieces, and Swiss chard, and cook for 15 minutes. Drain the vegetables. Using a hand-held immersion (stick) blender or food processor, blend the cooked vegetables to a puree.

Warm the broth in a pan and add 2 tablespoons of the pureed vegetables. Add the baby rice or cereal powder, mixing well with a whisk to keep from forming lumps.

Remove the pan from the heat. Transfer to a deep bowl or soup plate. Add the egg yolk and mix well, making sure that it is cooked through by the heat of the soup. Season with the olive oil and serve. Do not add salt.

Equipment needed:
Paring knife, saucepan, fine-mesh strainer, hand-held immersion (stick) blender or food processor, small stainless steel whisk.

A new vegetable each week:
There is no rush to introduce new foods into your child's diet. It is best to offer one new vegetable every four or five days at most. Once your child has accepted the new flavor without signs of allergies, you can continue experimenting until you have tested a good number of seasonal vegetables.

When you reach this point, you can invent new flavor combinations. This creamy soup, for instance, uses only green vegetables, while others can make use of orange or white vegetables. Each color indicates the presence of different nutrients, all of which are important for a baby's growth.

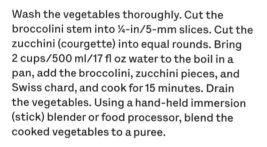

Recipes for 8 to 24 months

Creamy pumpkin, carrot, and orange soup with turkey

preparation time: 15 minutes
cooking time: 20 minutes
makes: one portion

· 1 small carrot
· ⅛ cup/30 g/1 oz diced pumpkin or butternut
  squash flesh
· 1 small thyme sprig
· ⅜ cup/50 g/2 oz leftover cooked turkey
· 1 cup/240 ml/8 fl oz vegetable broth (stock)
  (see page 58)
· 2 tbsp instant baby rice or cereal powder
  of your choice
· 1 tbsp orange juice
· 1 tsp extra virgin olive oil

Peel the carrot, cut off the ends, and thinly slice.
Wash the vegetables and thyme thoroughly.
Put the vegetables and thyme into a pan, cover
with at least 2 in (5 cm) of water, bring to a boil,
and cook for 15 minutes.

Drain the vegetables, then remove and discard
the thyme. Using a food processor, blend the
cooked vegetables with the cooked turkey
until smooth.

Warm the broth (stock) in a pan. Add the
baby rice or cereal powder, whisking to keep
from forming lumps. Stir through the pureed
vegetables and turkey.

Remove the pan from the heat. Transfer to
a deep bowl or soup plate. Season with the
orange juice and olive oil, mix, and serve.
Do not add any salt.

Equipment needed:
Vegetable peeler, paring knife, pan, fine-mesh
strainer, food processor, saucepan, small
stainless steel whisk.

Refrigerating baby food:
The suggestion that you don't store baby food
in the refrigerator doesn't mean the food goes
off quickly; it simply means that it's so fast and
easy to make that you don't have to stock up.
However, it may happen that after you have
prepared a meal, your baby has no desire to
even try it because of tiredness or not feeling
well. In that case, don't throw it away. Put
it into an airtight container and put it in the
refrigerator. You could try offering it again at
the next mealtime after reheating, but do use
within 24 hours.

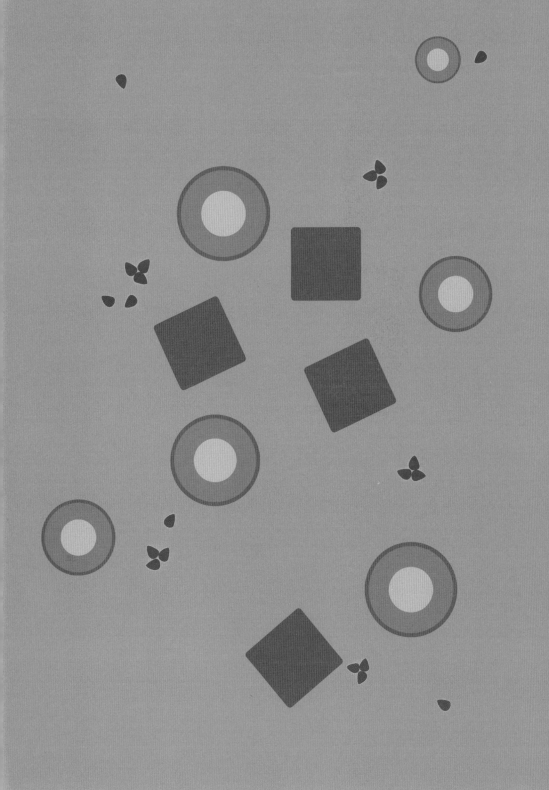

Baby's first pasta sauce

preparation time: 15 minutes
cooking time: 30 minutes
makes: eight to ten portions of sauce and
one portion of pasta

- 3 cups/1 kg/2 lb 4 oz ripe vine tomatoes
- 4 basil leaves
- 1 tbsp frozen or fresh soffritto mixture, made
  up from diced carrot, celery, and onion
- 2 tbsp soup pasta with a suitable shape for
  the baby's age
- 1 tsp extra virgin olive oil
- 1 tsp grated hard cheese, such as Parmesan

Wash and slice the tomatoes. Wash, dry, and tear up the basil leaves by hand. Combine with the soffritto mixture in a non-stick skillet (frying pan). Place over the heat and bring to the boil. Continue to cook over a high heat for about 20 minutes, stirring frequently. When the sauce thickens, remove from the heat and puree using a hand-held immersion (stick) blender or a food processor.

This will make 2 cups/450 g/1 lb of sauce, which can be stored in the refrigerator for up to 24 hours or frozen for up to three months in individual portions in an ice-cube tray.

Bring 2 cups/500 ml/17 fl oz water to the boil in a pan, add the pasta, and cook for 4 minutes or according to the directions on the packaging. Do not add salt. Drain, mix with 2 tablespoons sauce, season with the olive oil and grated cheese, and serve.

Equipment needed:
Non-stick skillet (frying pan), wooden spoon, hand-held immersion (stick) blender or food processor, ice-cube tray, saucepan with lid, strainer.

Stocking the freezer:
Make the most of the summer by preparing large quantities of tomato sauce to freeze and have ready to use over the winter months. Use the much riper, fleshier, and tastier tomatoes that those found in winter.

To freeze the sauce, use ice-cube trays with separate compartments. This will allow you to take out the portion you need each time without having to thaw out the entire tray.

Baby's first pasta carbonara

preparation time: 5 minutes
cooking time: 4 minutes
makes: one portion

· 1 cup/240 ml/8 fl oz vegetable broth (stock)
  (see page 58)
· 2 tbsp short angel hair soup noodles
· 1 small egg yolk
· 1 tsp grated hard cheese, such as Parmesan
· 1 tsp extra virgin olive oil

Bring the vegetable broth (stock) to the boil in a pan, add the noodles, and cook for 4 minutes or the time indicated in the packet directions.

In the meantime, use a fork to beat the very fresh egg yolk with the grated cheese in a deep plate until only slightly runny.

Drain the noodles and, while still steaming hot, immediately add the noodles to the plate with the beaten egg and cheese. Mix everything very well until the noodles are evenly coated and the heat from the noodles cooks the egg yolk. Mix in the olive oil and serve, making sure that the egg yolk is cooked through by the heat of the pasta. Do not add salt.

Equipment needed:
Saucepan, fork, grater, fine-mesh strainer.

Start with half an egg yolk:
This first version of the classic pasta carbonara uses only the yolk of a small egg, which can be introduced to infants in the eleventh month. If you have a large egg at home, separate the yolk onto a plate and beat with a fork. Remove one or two teaspoons of yolk from the plate and mix the rest with the grated cheese. Because a high protein intake is not recommended for children under the age of 12 months, just a very small amount of grated cheese is added. Make sure you use only the best quality and freshest of eggs when feeding your baby.

Green semolina with cooked ham

preparation time: 5 minutes
cooking time: 25 minutes
makes: one portion

- 1½ cups/60 g/2 oz beet greens (beetroot tops)
- ¼ cup/30 g/1 oz diced, lean, cooked ham
- 1 cup/240 ml/8 fl oz vegetable broth (stock)
  (see page 58)
- 4–5 tbsp instant semolina
- 1 tsp extra virgin olive oil

Clean the beet greens (beetroot tops), removing the roots and harder stems. Wash under running water until there are no traces of soil.

Bring 4 cups/1 liter/34 fl oz of water to a boil in a pan and add the beet greens. Cook for 10–15 minutes, then drain and puree in a food processor.

After removing any fatty parts, grind the ham in the food processor.

Warm the broth in a saucepan and add the pureed beet greens and the semolina, mixing with a whisk to keep from forming lumps.

Remove the pan from the heat and stir through the ham. Transfer to a small plate. Season with the olive oil, and serve.

Equipment needed:
Paring knife, pan with a lid, saucepan, fine-mesh strainer, food processor, small stainless steel whisk.

Ensuring baby's food stays warm:
Many babies take a long time to eat. As a result, the food gets cold and may become less appetizing. Some babies will prefer food cold, but if you need to reheat it, just add a little more liquid and warm through in the saucepan. Alternatively, you can use a microwave to reheat food, but always check the temperature and stir thoroughly to make sure there are no hot spots before serving.

Baby rice with turnip, potato, and chicken

preparation time: 5 minutes
cooking time: 30 minutes
makes: one portion

· 1 new potato
· 1 small turnip
· ⅜ cup/50 g/1¾ oz leftover cooked
  chicken, sliced
· 1 cup/240 ml/8 fl oz vegetable or chicken
  broth (stock) (see page 58)
· 4–5 tbsp instant baby rice
· 1 tsp extra virgin olive oil

Peel the potato and turnip, wash thoroughly, and cut into ½-in (1-cm) dice. Put into a pan and cover with at least 2 in (5 cm) of water. Cover with the lid and cook for about 20–25 minutes.

Drain the potato and turnip well. Using a hand-held immersion (stick) blender or food processor, puree the drained vegetables with the cooked chicken until smooth.

Warm the broth in a saucepan and add the instant baby rice, mixing with a whisk to keep from forming lumps. Stir through the pureed vegetables and chicken.

Remove the pan from the heat. Transfer to a small plate. Season with the olive oil, and serve. Do not add any salt.

Equipment needed:
Vegetable peeler, paring knife, pan with lid, saucepan, fine-mesh strainer, hand-held immersion (stick) blender or food processor, small stainless steel whisk.

Leftover meat and vegetables:
When you roast lamb or other meats for your own dinner, avoid seasoning the meat so that you can feed some of the leftovers to your baby. Similarly, when you cook vegetables keep any leftovers for pureeing and adding to your baby's meals. Just make sure that when you cook vegetables, you do not add any salt to the water.

Egg and zucchini soup

preparation time: 5 minutes
cooking time: 5 minutes
makes: one portion

· 1 medium zucchini (courgette)
· 1 cup/240 ml/8 fl oz vegetable broth
  (see page 58)
· 2 tbsp soup pasta with a suitable shape
  for the baby's age
· 1 small egg yolk
· 1 tsp extra virgin olive oil

Wash the zucchini (courgette) thoroughly and cut off the ends. Using a box grater, shred the zucchini into thin threads.

Bring the broth to a boil in a saucepan and add the zucchini threads. Wait a few minutes and add the pasta. Cook for 4 minutes or the time indicated on the packet. Remove from the heat and add the egg yolk, whisking briskly to incorporate evenly.

Transfer to a small plate, season with the olive oil, mix again, and serve, making sure that the egg yolk is cooked through by the heat of the soup.

Equipment needed:
Paring knife, box grater, saucepan, small stainless steel whisk.

Only a teaspoon:
Unless you have a family history of food allergies, cooked egg yolk can be introduced into dishes. If you are concerned about potential allergies, consult your pediatrician Start by adding only a teaspoon of yolk to your baby's food, then gradually increase the amount until you can use a whole cooked yolk to replace meat or fish once a week. Cooked egg white can be introduced from the age of 12 months.

Pasta with beef ragù

preparation time: 5 minutes
cooking time: 10 minutes
makes: one portion

· ⅓ cup/50 g/2 oz leftover cooked beef
· 2 tbsp tomato sauce (see page 110,
  baby's first pasta sauce)
· 1 small rosemary sprig, washed
· 1 cup/240 ml/8 fl oz vegetable broth (stock)
  (see page 58) or water
· 2 tbsp soup pasta with a suitable shape for
  the baby's age
· 1 tsp extra virgin olive oil

Grind the cooked beef in a food processor and
then put in a small saucepan with the tomato
sauce and rosemary. Place over a medium heat
for 2–3 minutes to allow the flavors to infuse.
Remove and discard the rosemary sprig.

Meanwhile, bring the broth (stock) or water
to a boil in a saucepan with a lid, and cook the
soup pasta for 4 minutes or the time indicated
in the packet directions. Drain the pasta and
add to the pan with the beef ragù.

Remove the pan from the heat. Transfer to a
small plate. Season with the olive oil, mix, and
serve. Do not add any salt.

Equipment needed:
Food processor, saucepan, pan with lid,
strainer.

Individual portions:
To make life easier, prepare a large batch of
this ragù and freeze it in individual ¼-cup/
50-g/2-oz portions so that they are to hand
when needed. To thaw, put a portion in the
refrigerator the night before, or put it directly
into a pan and thaw over a low heat, stirring
frequently.

Rice, parsley, potato, and beef

preparation time: 5 minutes
cooking time: 15 minutes
makes: one portion

· 2 oz/50 g leftover cooked beef
· 4 parsley leaves
· 1 cup/240 ml/8 fl oz vegetable broth (stock)
  (see page 58)
· 1 small potato, boiled and peeled
· 2 tbsp instant baby rice
· 1 tsp extra virgin olive oil

Grind the cooked beef in a food processor.
Wash, dry, and finely chop the parsley.

Warm the broth (stock) in a pan. Cut the potato
into small dice, and add to the pan with the
broth. As soon as the potato turns soft, mash
with a fork. Add the baby rice and cook for
5 minutes, stirring frequently with a wooden
spoon. Next, add the ground beef and mix well.

Remove the pan from the heat. Transfer to
a small plate. Season with the olive oil and
chopped parsley, mix, and serve. Do not add
any salt.

Equipment needed:
Paring knife, saucepan, fork, wooden spoon,
food processor.

Cooked meat:
The next time you roast meat, make sure you do
not add any salt or pepper and save a few slices
to make recipes like this one to feed to your
baby. Sliced cooked meat can be kept in the
refrigerator for two days or ground and frozen
until needed.

Easter lamb soup with spring vegetables

preparation time: 20 minutes
cooking time: 30 minutes
makes: one portion

- · 1 tbsp shelled fava (broad) beans, fresh or frozen
- · ½ cleaned artichoke heart
- · 1 tbsp shelled peas, fresh or frozen
- · 2 parsley leaves, washed
- · ⅓ cup/50 g/2 oz leftover cooked lamb
- · 2 tbsp instant baby rice or cereal powder
- · 1 tsp extra virgin olive oil

Blanch the fava (broad) beans in boiling water and peel. Dice the artichoke.

Bring 2 cups/500 ml/17 fl oz water to the boil in a pan, add the fava beans, diced artichoke, peas, and parsley leaves. Reduce the heat and simmer for 15–20 minutes.

Drain the vegetables, reserving the broth (stock). Puree the vegetables with the lamb using a hand-held immersion (stick) blender or food processor until smooth.

Heat up 1 cup/240 ml/8 fl oz of the reserved vegetable broth in a saucepan, add the baby rice or cereal powder, and cook for 4 minutes or the time indicated on the packet. Add the pureed lamb and vegetables to the soup, and mix well.

Remove from the heat. Transfer to a small plate. Season with the olive oil, mix again, and serve.

Equipment needed:
Pan, saucepan, steamer basket, food processor.

A little fatty, but less allergenic:
Lamb is less likely to cause an allergic reaction than other meats, but tends to be fatty. For leaner, tender meat, use ground lamb from a chop or tenderloin, or use commercially available pureed lamb.

Batch cooking:
Double up the recipe so that you use a whole artichoke and freeze the leftover portion for later use.

Semolina with artichoke, asparagus, and cod

preparation time: 15 minutes
cooking time: 20 minutes
makes: one portion

· 1 artichoke
· juice of ½ lemon
· 4 asparagus tips
· ¼ cup/50 g/2 oz cleaned and skinless cod, sliced
· 1 cup/240 ml/8 fl oz vegetable or fish broth (stock) (see pages 58 or 88)
· 4–5 tbsp instant semolina
· 1 tsp extra virgin olive oil
· a few parsley leaves, washed and finely chopped

Remove the harder outer leaves from the artichoke and cut off the stem. Trim the tip, then halve the heart and remove the choke. Cut the artichoke heart into thin slices and soak in water with the lemon juice to prevent oxidizing. Wash the asparagus tips and cut into dice.

Put the asparagus and artichoke into a steamer basket and steam for 20 minutes until tender. After the vegetables have been steaming for 12 minutes, add the fish slices to the steamer.

Using a hand-held immersion (stick) blender or food processor, puree the vegetables and fish until smooth. If necessary, loosen with a little of the cooking liquid.

Warm the broth (stock) in a pan and add the semolina, whisking to keep from forming lumps. Stir through the pureed fish and vegetables.

Remove the pan from the heat. Transfer to a small plate. Season with the olive oil and parsley, mix, and serve. Do not add salt.

Equipment needed:
Paring knife, bowl, lemon squeezer, steamer basket, pan with lid, hand-held immersion (stick) blender or food processor, saucepan, small stainless steel whisk.

The best part of the asparagus:
In order to easily remove the woody part of the asparagus spear, hold one end with your right hand and the other with your left hand. Bend the spear—which should be very fresh and cold from the refrigerator—flexing it like a bow until it breaks. Discard the hard part of the stalk, or peel and clean to use for another dish. The remaining tip, which is the tender part, is used for this recipe.

Cream of rice with fava beans, peas, and trout

preparation time: 10 minutes
cooking time: 25 minutes
makes: one portion

· 1 tbsp fresh or frozen fava (broad) beans
· 1 tbsp fresh or frozen peas
· 1 thin scallion (spring onion), white part only
· 2 basil leaves, washed and dried
· ¼ cup/50 g/2 oz trout fillet, cleaned and skinless
· 1 cup/240 ml/8 fl oz vegetable broth (stock)
· 4–5 tbsp baby rice powder
· 1 tsp extra virgin olive oil

Wash the fava (broad) beans, peas, and scallion (spring onion) thoroughly. Wash and dry the basil leaves. Slice the scallion. Bring 4 cups/ 1 liter/34 fl oz of water to a boil in a pan, add the vegetables, partially cover with the lid, and cook for 15 minutes. Do not add any salt. Drain. Peel the beans and set aside.

Wash the trout fillet and remove any bones with tweezers. Steam the trout for 6–7 minutes. Using a food processor, puree the trout, cooked vegetables, and basil leaves. For more developed infants, you can cut the fish into small pieces and puree only the vegetables.

Warm the broth in a pan. Add the baby rice powder, whisking to keep from forming lumps. Stir through the pureed fish and vegetables, and mix well.

Remove the pan from the heat. Transfer to a small plate. Season with the olive oil, and serve. Do not add any salt.

Equipment needed:
Paring knife, pan with lid, fine-mesh strainer, tweezers, steamer basket, food processor, saucepan, small stainless steel whisk.

Store ready to use in the freezer:
This spring dish uses fava beans, peas, and scallion, but you can vary the vegetables according to market availability or alternate with others. After pureeing, take out only the 2–3 tablespoons needed to mix with the fish, and store the remainder in the refrigerator for 24 hours or in the freezer, portioned into suitable containers.

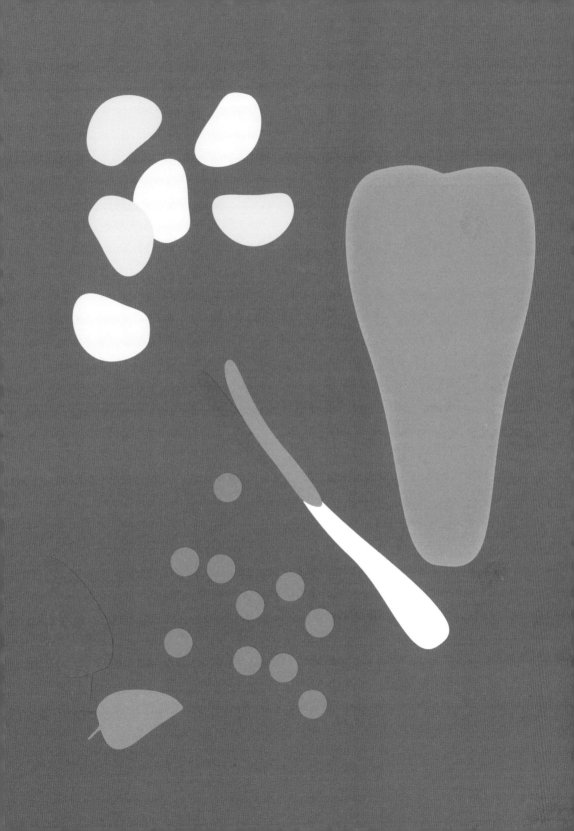

Baby's first Mediterranean couscous

preparation time: 5 minutes
cooking time: 5 minutes
makes: one portion

· ½ cup/125 ml/4 fl oz vegetable broth (stock) (see page 58)
· 2 tbsp couscous
· 1 ripe vine tomato
· 1 small zucchini (courgette)
· 1 tbsp grated hard cheese, such as Parmesan
· 1 tsp extra virgin olive oil

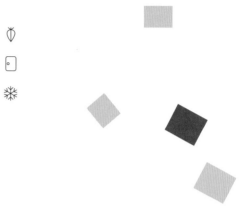

Warm the vegetable broth (stock) in a pan. Put the couscous into a bowl, pour over the hot broth to just cover the couscous and leave until it absorbs all the liquid.

Wash the tomato and score the base with a cross. Blanch in boiling water for 30 seconds, then drain, peel, and cut into quarters. Scoop out the seeds and finely chop the flesh. Wash the zucchini (courgette), trim the ends, and finely chop.

Heat 4 tablespoons of the remaining broth in a small pan and add the finely chopped zucchini. Simmer for 2–3 minutes over a medium heat, then add the tomato and cook for a further 2–3 minutes, adding more broth if the mixture becomes too dry.

Transfer the couscous to a small plate. Stir though the cooked vegetables. Season with the grated cheese and oil, mix, and serve. Do not add salt.

Equipment needed:
Saucepan, bowl, paring knife, small pan, wooden spoon.

Pleasing everybody:
Couscous is often something the whole family enjoys, so you can make a larger batch following the same instructions and using the ratio of 1 cup of couscous to 1 cup of warm broth. Once you have set aside the baby's portion, you can season the rest in different ways.

Babies also love plain dishes. Try making couscous simply seasoned with 1 teaspoon of olive oil and 1 tablespoon of a grated hard cheese, such as Parmesan. Complete the meal with some vegetable puree or grated fruit.

Mashed potatoes with ham

preparation time: 10 minutes
cooking time: 25 minutes
makes: one portion

· 1 small potato
· ½ cup/125 ml/4 fl oz made-up formula milk
· 1 tsp extra virgin olive oil
· ¼ cup/30 g/1 oz diced, lean, cooked ham

Peel, wash, and cut the potato into quarters. Put into a pan, cover with at least 2 in (5 cm) of water, bring to a boil, cover with a lid, and continue to cook for 20 minutes or until the potato is tender and can be crushed easily with a fork.

Using a slotted spoon, remove the potato from the pan and transfer to a soup plate. Warm the formula milk and pour over the potato, then mash together with a fork until smooth. Briefly whisk the mashed potato, add the oil, and continue whisking until smooth and fluffy.

Grind the ham in a food processor and stir through the mashed potato.

Equipment needed:
Vegetable peeler, paring knife, pan with lid, slotted spoon, small stainless steel whisk, food processor.

No meal without cereal:
To complete the meal, serve a cream of cereal, pasta, or a simple rice with vegetable broth (see page 58) alongside. Alternatively round off the meal with some grated fruit and a mashed sugar-free teething biscuit (rusk).

Bread, egg, tomato, and grated cheese

preparation time: 5 minutes
cooking time: 5 minutes
makes: one portion

· 1 cup/240 ml/8 fl oz vegetable broth (stock)
  (see page 58)
· ½ cup/30 g/1 oz crusty bread
· 2 tbsp tomato sauce (see page 110, baby's
  first pasta sauce)
· 1 tsp extra virgin olive oil
· 1 small egg yolk
· 1 tsp grated hard cheese, such as Parmesan

Warm the vegetable broth (stock) in a pan. Break the bread into pieces and arrange slightly overlapped in a deep bowl or soup plate. Pour the hot broth over the bread and let swell.

Dot the bread with the tomato sauce and oil. Carefully spread the sauce, lightly pressing with the back of a spoon, so that it soaks all the way through the bread.

Add the egg yolk to the bowl or plate, then press with the spoon to break the yolk and flavor the bread. Sprinkle with grated cheese and serve, making sure that the egg yolk is cooked through by the heat of the sauce.

Equipment needed:
Saucepan, spoon, grater.

A tasty dish that melts in the mouth:
This super-quick dish is very tasty and popular with babies who prefer soft food. The bread swells as it soaks up the broth, acquiring a pudding-like consistency that slides into the mouth and melts against the palate. Use a grated hard cheese such as Parmesan for the first time, and then, if your baby likes well-flavored dishes, try replacing it with Gruyère. You can also use Pecorino cheese, which features in the original Sardinian recipe, but only after the age of 12 months. Pecorino is a tasty but very salty cheese, so it isn't really suitable for very small infants.

Soft fish balls
in vegetable broth

preparation time: 15 minutes
cooking time: 30 minutes
makes: two portions

· 1 potato
· 1 parsley sprig, washed and dried
· ½ cup/100 g/4 oz fresh cod or hake, ground
· 1 tbsp dried breadcrumbs
· 1 cup/240 ml/8 fl oz vegetable broth (stock)
  (see page 58)
· 2 tbsp tomato sauce (see page 110, baby's
  first pasta sauce)
· 1 tsp extra virgin olive oil

Peel and halve the potato. Put into a pan covered by at least 2 in (5 cm) of water, cover with the lid, and cook for 15 minutes or until the potato can be easily pricked with a fork. Drain well and mash with a masher or potato ricer.

Clean, wash, and dry the parsley. Clean the fish and carefully remove any bones with tweezers. Steam the fish for 5 minutes. Let cool and puree in a food processor together with the parsley.

Transfer the pureed fish to a bowl, add the mashed potato, and mix until thick and smooth. If the mixture is too soft, add a few breadcrumbs and mix again.

Wet your hands and shape the mixture into hazelnut-sized balls, and dredge in the breadcrumbs.

Warm the broth, add the tomato sauce and half of the fish balls, then cook for 1 minute. Season with the olive oil and serve lukewarm.

Equipment needed:
Vegetable peeler, paring knife, pan with lid, masher or potato ricer, tweezers, steamer basket, food processor, freezer bags.

Only lean fish:
You can use any white-fleshed fish provided all skin and bones have been removed. Do not mash the potato in a food processor. The starch is torn out by the blades, turning it gluey. If you do not have a masher or potato ricer, use a fork and remove any lumps by mixing with the fish.

This recipe makes two portions of fish balls, so freeze half of them for future use. When you want to cook them, just bring some vegetable broth to a boil, add the fish balls, and wait for the liquid to come back to a boil, then cook for 1 minute.

Sweet semolina with apple

preparation time: 5 minutes
cooking time: 15 minutes
makes: one portion

· 1 eating apple (such as Golden Delicious
  or Gala)
· 1 cup/240 ml/8 fl oz made-up formula milk
· 4–5 tbsp instant semolina

Peel, wash, and cut the apple into quarters. Remove the core and cut into ½-in (1-cm) dice. Put in a saucepan with 1 cup/240 ml/8 fl oz water and cook over a low heat for about 15 minutes.

Towards the end of the cooking time for the apple, warm the formula milk in a pan. Add the semolina, mixing with a whisk to keep from forming lumps.

Once cooked, drain the apple. Using a hand-held immersion (stick) blender or a food processor, blend the apple to a puree.

Stir the apple puree through the semolina. Transfer to a small plate and serve.

Equipment needed:
Vegetable peeler, paring knife, saucepan, fine-mesh strainer, small stainless steel whisk, hand-held immersion (stick) blender or food processor.

Substitute cereal for the semolina:
This afternoon snack can also be made using a commercially available cereal and milk product instead of semolina. Many different kinds are available in stores. If you choose one containing ground teething biscuits (rusks), you must dissolve it in water instead of formula milk and following the packet directions.

Yogurt, ricotta, and persimmon mousse

preparation time: 5 minutes
cooking time: none
makes: one portion

· 1 ripe persimmon (sharon fruit)
· 1½ tbsp ricotta cheese
· ⅓ cup/100 ml/3½ fl oz full-fat plain yogurt

Peel the persimmon (sharon fruit). Using a hand-held immersion (stick) blender or food processor, blend the fruit with the ricotta, gradually adding the yogurt a spoonful at a time, until smooth.

Transfer to a bowl and serve with spoon.

Equipment needed:
Paring knife, hand-held immersion (stick) blender or food processor.

Also use other seasonal fruit:
You can make this afternoon snack with any fruit, provided it is suitable for infants under the age of 12 months. Blending the ricotta with fruit that has a high water content, such as persimmon and melon, produces a puree with a creamy consistency. However, blending the ricotta with drier fruit, such as apple, results in a softer consistency. A creamy puree will be smoother and incorporate better with the yogurt, a product that is high in protein, calcium, phosphorous, and probiotics.

Recipes for 8 to 24 months

Cream of pumpkin with cinnamon

preparation time: 10 minutes
cooking time: 15 minutes
makes: one portion

· ½ cup/50 g/1¾ oz diced pumpkin or butternut
  squash flesh
· ¾ cup/200 ml/7 fl oz made-up formula milk
· a pinch of ground cinnamon

Put the diced pumpkin or squash into a non-stick saucepan, and cover with the formula milk. Bring to the boil, cover with the lid, and continue to cook over a medium heat until the squash starts to break down, about 10 minutes. Add a few tablespoons of water if needed.

When the pumpkin or squash is soft, remove the pan from the heat and add the cinnamon. Using a hand-held immersion (stick) blender or food processor, puree until smooth. Let cool, then transfer to a small plate and serve.

Equipment needed:
Paring knife, non-stick saucepan with lid, hand-held immersion (stick) blender or food processor.

High in vitamin A:
Pumpkin or squash is used as the main ingredients in certain fall (autumn) desserts. Because it is low in sodium, it is perfectly suited for less-developed babies who aren't allowed salt in their diet. Plus it is one of the vegetables, after carrots, that contain the highest amount of vitamin A, which strengthens the retina and improves night vision.

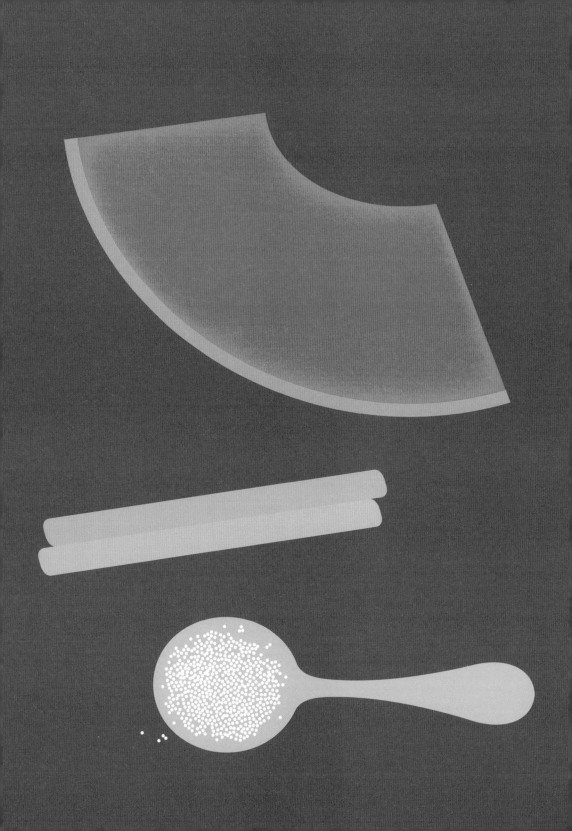

Pear compote with cookies and persimmon sauce

preparation time: 5 minutes
cooking time: 15 minutes
makes: one portion

· 1 ripe eating pear, such as Bartlett (Williams), Conference, or Comice
· ½ vanilla bean (pod)
· ½ ripe persimmon (sharon fruit)
· 2 gluten-free, dairy-free, and egg-free cookies (see page 156)
· 2 tbsp pear juice

Wash, peel, core, and dice the pear, then put into a small pan. Split the ½ vanilla bean (pod) in half lengthways and add to the pan along with 4 tablespoons of water. Place over a medium heat and cook until the pear begins to break down, about 10 minutes, stirring frequently.

Remove the pan from the heat, and remove and discard the vanilla bean. Using a hand-held immersion (stick) blender or food processor, puree the pear together with the cooking water. Wash, peel, and puree the persimmon (sharon fruit).

Arrange the cookies on a small plate and soak them with the pear juice. Cover the cookies with the pureed pear compote and pureed persimmon sauce and serve immediately.

Equipment needed:
Vegetable peeler, paring knife, saucepan, hand-held immersion (stick) blender or food processor.

Cereal with cheese:
You can enrich this afternoon snack by spreading a tablespoon of yogurt or cream cheese over the pureed pear before adding the persimmon sauce. Depending on the season, you can substitute the persimmon with another permitted fruit, such as peach, apricot, and plum.

Rice pudding with plum

preparation time: 5 minutes
cooking time: 8 minutes
makes: one portion

· 1 cup/240 ml/8 fl oz made-up formula milk
· 2 tbsp instant baby rice
· 1 very ripe plum

Warm the formula milk in a pan. As soon as it comes to a boil, add the baby rice. Cook over a low heat, stirring frequently, for about 6–8 minutes.

Meanwhile, thoroughly wash the plum, and remove the pit (stone). Using a hand-held immersion (stick) blender or food processor, blend to a puree.

Remove the pan from the heat. Transfer the rice to a small bowl, and let cool slightly. Add the pureed plum, mix, and serve lukewarm or at room temperature. Do not add any sugar.

Equipment needed:
Saucepan, paring knife, hand-held immersion (stick) blender or food processor, small bowl.

Cool and naturally sweet:
You can substitute the plum with an apricot, small peach, or banana, or with commercially available pureed fruit.

If you decide to use ripe seasonal fruit, its natural sweetness will flavor the pudding without the need to add any sweetener.

If you are feeling adventurous, try flavoring the pudding with a pinch of ground cinnamon, for infants older than 10 or 11 months.

In summer, babies feeling the heat will certainly appreciate a cool afternoon snack. Make the pudding in advance and cool for a few hours in the refrigerator. Serve cool, but not chilled.

Recipes for 8 to 24 months

Seasonal fruit puree with orange juice

preparation time: 5 minutes
cooking time: none
makes: one portion

· ⅜–½ cup/70–100 g/2½–3½ oz fresh,
   seasonal fruit of your choice
· 1 orange

Wash, peel, and cut up the seasonal fruit of your choice. Wash and squeeze the orange to extract the juice.

Put the fruit into a food processor or blender, add the orange juice, and then blend to a smooth puree.

Transfer the fruit puree to a small bowl and serve with a spoon.

Equipment needed:
Paring knife, lemon squeezer, food processor or blender.

Seasonal fruit mix:
Some possible fruit combinations include apple, pear, and banana; apricot and peach; banana and persimmon (sharon fruit); melon and watermelon; plum and grape (flesh only, seeds and skin removed); banana and pineapple; and banana and mango.

It's useful to remember that fruit purees should always be made with fresh, very ripe, seasonal fruit, chosen from those ones that are permissible for this age group (see pages 49 and 53).

Cream cheese with peach and apricot puree

preparation time: 5 minutes
cooking time: none
makes: one portion

- ½ small peach
- 1 small apricot
- 1½ tbsp Greek yogurt or pasteurized soft cream cheese, such as Philadelphia or Petit-Suisse

Wash the fruit thoroughly. Peel the peach, and remove the pits (stones) from both the peach and the apricot. Using a hand-held immersion (stick) blender or food processor, puree the fruit until smooth.

Put the cream or soft cheese in a bowl and work with a wooden spoon until soft and creamy.

Pour the pureed fruit over the cheese and serve, taking a little cheese with a small amount of the fruit puree with each spoonful.

Equipment needed:
Paring knife, hand-held immersion (stick) blender or food processor, mixing bowl, wooden spoon.

Cream cheese:
Whenever cream cheese for infants of this age is referred to, this means pasteurized soft cheese, such as Philadelphia and Petit-Suisse. Full-fat cheeses and dairy products are recommended for children under 2 years as they need the energy from fats to fuel growth.

Yogurt mousse with banana and clementine juice

preparation time: 5 minutes
cooking time: none
makes: one portion

· ½ banana
· ⅜ cup/100 g/3½ oz Greek yogurt
· juice of 1 clementine

Peel the banana and cut the fruit into slices. Combine the yogurt, sliced banana, and clementine juice in a blender or food processor and blend until smooth and fluffy.

Transfer to a small bowl and serve with a spoon.

Freeze the leftover sliced banana for future use.

Equipment needed:
Paring knife, blender or food processor.

Nutritious and refreshing:
This is a simplified version of a smoothie, a rich milkshake-like drink made with fresh fruit and ice, with added milk, yogurt, ice cream, and spices, cocoa, peanut butter, or whatever takes the maker's fancy. A combination of milk with fruit; yogurt, milk, and fruit; or only yogurt with pureed fruit will always make a healthy, nutritious, and refreshing afternoon snack.

Blueberry, banana, and orange yogurt milkshake

preparation time: 10 minutes
cooking time: none
makes: four portions

· 2 cups/200 g/7 oz blueberries
· 1 unwaxed lemon
· 1 ripe banana
· 1 orange
· ¾ cup/200 g/7 oz full-fat plain yogurt
· ½ cup/100 ml/3½ fl oz full-fat (whole) milk
· 2 tbsp rolled oats

Rinse and dry the blueberries, setting aside 30 berries to squash and serve on the side. Rinse the lemon, grate the zest into a bowl, and then squeeze and strain the juice into another bowl. Peel the banana, then cut the fruit into rounds and soak the slices in the lemon juice to keep them from turning brown. Squeeze the orange and strain the juice into a jug.

Combine the blueberries, banana, orange juice, yogurt, milk, and oats in a blender or food processor and blend until smooth, about 2 minutes.

Pour a quarter of the milkshake into a cup or beaker. Sprinkle a little grated lemon zest over the top and serve immediately, with a handful of squashed whole berries for your baby to feed themselves by hand.

This recipe makes enough milkshake for four servings, so it is ideal if you have a large family or friends over. Otherwise, use the mixture to make fruity yogurt ice pops (see right).

Equipment needed:
Lemon zester, fine-mesh strainer, paring knife, lemon squeezer, blender or food processor, baby cup or beaker.

Fruity yogurt ice pops:
The milkshake mixture can be used to make delicious frozen yogurt ice pops, which are loved by young and old alike. Add the whole blueberries to the milkshake mixture and then pour into individual ice pop molds. Insert the ice pop stick or handle into each mold and freeze for at least 4–5 hours. For an occasional treat, make a creamier mixture with a consistency more like ice cream, substitute the whole (full-fat) milk with the same quantity of heavy (double) cream.

Gluten-free, dairy-free, and egg-free cookies

preparation time: 20 minutes
cooking time: 15 minutes
makes: about 40 small cookies

· 2 ripe bananas
· 3 tbsp mild olive oil
· a few drops of vanilla extract (optional)
· 1 cup/150 g/5⅓ oz fine cornmeal (polenta), plus extra for dusting
· 1½ cups/150 g/5⅓ oz almond flour or finely ground almonds

Preheat the oven to 350°F/180°C/160°C fan/gas 4 and line one or more baking sheets with parchment paper.

Peel the bananas and mash the fruit in a bowl, add the olive oil and vanilla, if using, then mix well. Combine the cornmeal (polenta) and almond flour in another bowl. Make a well in the center and add the banana mixture. Mix with a silicone spatula, then knead to a smooth dough on a work surface lightly dusted with cornmeal.

Divide the dough into four equal pieces. Roll out one piece of dough to a thickness of ¼ in (6 mm). Using a 1-in (3-cm) cutter, cut out 10 cookies. Lay the cookies on the lined baking sheets. Repeat with the remaining dough, or cover in plastic wrap and freeze for use later.

Bake the cookies in the preheated oven for 12–15 minutes or until the edges turn a light golden. Transfer to a wire rack and let cool.

Equipment needed:
Baking sheets, parchment paper, mixing bowls, silicone spatula, rolling pin, 1-in (3-cm) cookie cutter, wire cooling rack.

Alternative flavors:
When making these cookies for older infants, other ingredients can be added, such as ground spices (cinnamon or ginger), chocolate chips, chopped pine nuts or pistachios, or you can sprinkle the tops of the cookies with chopped hazelnuts just before baking.

Tip:
After baking, freeze the cookies in batches. To eat, take out of the freezer and leave to thaw until needed.

Seasonal produce

Spring

Fields and gardens come alive in the spring and suddenly the offering of fresh vegetables becomes rich and varied. Though spoiled for choice, you can familiarize yourself with the different varieties through advice on their nutritional value and simple instructions on the best ways to cook them.

Asparagus

Asparagus was prized in ancient Egypt, and was accurately described by both Cato and Pliny. There are more than 200 varieties of asparagus, distinguishable by their flavor and appearance, and include white asparagus, purple asparagus, as well as the classic green asparagus. All varieties are picked between late March and late June. Asparagus found in other seasons are either grown in greenhouses or imported.

Buying and storing:
Fresh asparagus spears have straight and tightly closed tips that can be cleanly snapped off. The stalks must be shiny, hard, flexible, and free of cracks. Wrap the asparagus spears in a damp cloth and store in the refrigerator for up to three to four days. Can be frozen.

Basic cooking:
Rinse the asparagus spears under cold running water. Place the asparagus in a steamer and cook for 8–10 minutes, depending on size. Puree the asparagus using a food processor or hand-held immersion (stick) blender. When your baby is old enough for finger foods, steam the asparagus spears, cut them into small pieces, and serve on a plate for them to feed themselves.

Green beans

Also known as string beans or snap beans, these are green beans picked in the pod before ripening, while still small and tender. They're harvested from May through September and are typically green, although the pod can also be yellow, in which case they're known as wax beans, and purple, known as purple beans. They are high in fiber, vitamin A and C, protein, and potassium, and are low in calories.

Buying and storing:
The pod has to be intact, firm, and bright in color, and snap cleanly when broken. The best ones are tender with a short string. They will keep in the refrigerator in a food storage bag for two to three days at most.

Basic cooking:
Rinse the green beans under cold running water. Trim off both ends from the beans. Place the beans in a steamer and cook for 3–5 minutes, or until tender. Puree the green beans using a food processor or hand-held immersion (stick) blender. When your baby is old enough for finger foods, steam the green beans, cut them into small pieces, and serve on a plate for them to feed themselves.

Peas

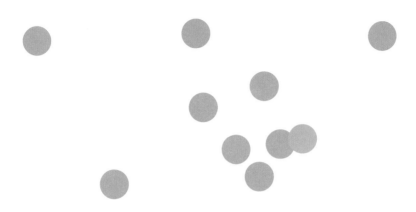

Peas are the seeds of a leguminous plant native to the Mediterranean region and Asia, but grown throughout the world. They are harvested in spring while still tender and sweet. They're among the most easily digested of the legumes and help to relieve constipation. Like many legumes, they contain proteins of reasonable biological value and small amounts of unsaturated fat. They are a great vegetable for babies.

Buying and storing:
The best peas come in plump, bright green pods that are firm when pressed. The pods come with small stems and contain at least five, well-formed, tender, and juicy peas. The whole pods will keep in the refrigerator for a couple of days, and shelled peas stored in an airtight container will keep for four to five days.

Basic cooking:
If using fresh peas, shell the peas to remove them from their pods. Place the peas in a steamer and cook for 3 minutes, or until tender. Alternatively, place the peas in a pan and boil for 3 minutes. Puree the peas using a food processor or hand-held immersion (stick) blender, adding a little of the cooking water if necessary. When your baby is old enough for a chunkier puree, steam the peas and crush them using a potato masher.

Scallions (Spring onions)

Scallion (spring onion) refers to the white onion that is found throughout the year and grown to be eaten fresh, but harvested when the bulb is still immature. Children can be introduced to it as a "baby" onion, although it is equally high in vitamins and minerals.

Buying and storing:
Scallions must be firm, free from spots or signs of rot, and with long green shoots. They can keep for a few days wrapped in a paper towel in the refrigerator.

Basic cooking:
Introduce this flavor to your baby by adding a little scallion to your chosen vegetables, cooked and pureed. Scallions can also be braised in a little oil together with other vegetables, such as peas, asparagus, and potatoes, and then pureed for your baby.

Spinach

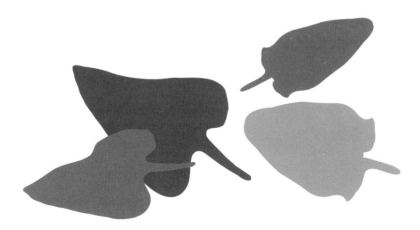

Available fresh at markets practically throughout the year, spinach is among the world's most widely produced vegetables. Spring varieties, such as Matador, are the most tender and flavorful. Spinach is considered to be quintessentially healthy because it's low in calories but high in dietary fiber, vitamins, and minerals. It has a remarkable iron content, which is better absorbed by the body when eaten cooked and seasoned with lemon juice.

Buying and storing:
Spinach leaves should be deep green, shiny, blemish-free, and not wilted. The stems should be firm and freshly cut, no longer than 4 in (10 cm). Wrapped in paper towels, spinach can be kept in the refrigerator for a few days. Once cooked, however, it should be eaten immediately.

Basic cooking:
If using fresh spinach, rinse the leaves under cold running water. Place the spinach in a steamer and cook for 3–5 minutes, or until tender. Puree the spinach using a food processor or hand-held immersion (stick) blender, adding a little of the cooking water if necessary.

Zucchini (Courgettes)

Zucchini (courgettes) are found in markets between April and September. Those found outside of this time are usually imported. Zucchini has high amounts of nutrients but few calories. It contains calcium, iron, potassium, phosphorous, vitamin C, and beta-carotene. Zucchini can be prepared in many different ways: fried, broiled (grilled), stuffed, gratinated, added to soups, pasta, and risotto dishes.

Buying and storing:
The best specimens are small or medium in size and have a shiny and smooth skin, without any marks. They are firm to touch, with a freshly cut stem. Zucchini can keep in the refrigerator for more than two days in a food storage bag to keep the moisture in.

Basic cooking:
Rinse the zucchini under cold running water. Trim off both ends from the zucchini and cut into slices. Place the zucchini in a steamer and cook for 5 minutes, depending on size. Puree the zucchini using a food processor or hand-held immersion (stick) blender, adding a little of the cooking water if necessary.

Coming into season in spring:

- asparagus
- beans
- bell peppers
- celery
- cucumbers
- eggplant (aubergine)
- garlic
- lettuce
- new potatoes
- Swiss chard
- tomatoes
- tropea red onions

Still available from winter:

Besides the vegetables grown throughout the year and those coming into season, there are still some winter vegetables available, that can be used to enhance the range of springtime offerings:

- artichokes
- broccoli
- fennel
- leeks
- radicchio

Summer

Brightly colored, ripe, and juicy, seasonal summer vegetables are a real treat to use in the kitchen. Now is the time to use them in delicious appetizers and tasty gratin dishes. Seek out the best of the summer produce at local markets, where they are fresh, plentiful, and economical.

Beans

These are the seeds, encased in a pod, of climbing leguminous plants. The most widespread of the more than 500 existing species was imported into Europe following the discovery of America. Beans are sold dried or cooked and preserved in a can. Fresh beans are only found in season from July through to October.

They are high in dietary fiber and contain reasonable amounts of protein (20–22 percent), phosphorous, potassium, sodium, magnesium, and iron. They are a good source of energy and are restorative. Beans have been known as "poor man's meat" for many years, and even today are considered a valid alternative to main course meat dishes.

Buying and storing:
Fresh beans should come in a firm and smooth pod, and they should be well-formed, plump, and uniform in size. However, they are typically sold in cans, frozen, or dried. When buying canned beans, check the label to make sure they do not contain sugar. Dried beans should be checked to make sure they are intact, without small holes or webs. It will then be necessary to soak them for about 12 hours to bring them back to life. Discard any that are still floating after this time. Fresh, shelled beans will keep in the refrigerator for three to four days. Dried and canned beans will keep in the pantry for up to one year.

Basic cooking:
Whether fresh or dried, after soaking in warm water, put the beans in a pan of cold water and cook over low heat for a couple of hours.

Bell peppers

The sweet bell pepper is actually the large and fleshy berry of a plant native to Central America. It can be yellow, red, or green, although the green ones are mostly immature red and yellow fruit, which means that it isn't uncommon to find variegated specimens.

Very low in calories, the bell pepper strengthens blood vessels, acts as an antioxidant agent, and stimulates the appetite. It's an excellent source of vitamin E, A, and C, which allows it to offer significant protection for the liver, heart, skin, and eyesight.

Buying and storing:
Fresh bell peppers have smooth and shiny skin, a regular shape, firmly attached stem, and crunchy flesh. They will keep for a few days in the refrigerator.

Basic cooking:
Bell pepper is delicious broiled (grilled) whole for 15–20 minutes, then peeled and seasoned with oil—a great vegetable introduce to an older baby.

Eggplant (Aubergines)

The eggplant (aubergine) is the large berry of a plant originating in Asia and introduced to the Mediterranean region by the Arabs during the Middle Ages. However, at the end of the sixteenth century, it was considered in the West to cause illness and insanity.

Eggplant is, however, low in calories and contains high amounts of potassium, phosphorous, and calcium. The eggplant has mild laxative properties, while it stimulates liver function and helps to lower blood cholesterol.

Buying and storing:
A good eggplant must be firm but soft to the touch, with smooth and shiny skin, plus a thick, green, and spiny stem. Smaller ones are the best. They will keep in the refrigerator for three to four days.

Basic cooking:
Roast half an eggplant with a little oil, scrape the soft flesh away from the skin, then give to your baby.

Lettuce

Although lettuce is grown throughout the year, the best varieties are those that come onto the market in the early summer. Lettuce is low in calories but high in vitamins and minerals. The darker leaves are a good source of vitamin B9, also known as folic acid, as well as carotenoids and iron.

Buying and storing:
The leaves should be fresh, crisp, with a white tuft at the point where the head was cut. Washed and dried, lettuce can keep in the refrigerator wrapped in a damp cloth for three or four days.

Basic cooking:
Lettuce can be cooked in vegetable soups and cream soups. Once your baby is older, the raw leaves can even be used as a wrapper or carrier for other ingredients made into a filling or a dip.

Tomatoes

This is one of the world's most widely cultivated fruits. It was introduced into Europe from Central America in the sixteenth century and initially used as an ornamental plant. It was the farmers of southern Italy, Spain, and other Mediterranean countries who realized it combined well with the traditional bread and onion, the base of their diet.

Tomatoes are now found throughout the year because they're grown in greenhouses, but those grown in the open air are picked from July through to October. They have large amounts of potassium and vitamin C, and the antioxidant properties of the lycopene and other carotenoids they contain make them good for healthy skin and eyesight.

Buying and storing:
Tomatoes should have a small and somewhat hard, dark green stem. Except for irregularly shaped field tomatoes, they should have a smooth, shiny, and unrippled skin, and flesh that is firm to the touch. Tomatoes shouldn't be stored in the refrigerator but at room temperature, above 50°F/10°C, where they will continue to ripen.

Basic cooking:
Although excellent raw, tomatoes can be turned into sauce (see page 110) for immediate use or to be stored and used in countless recipes.

Still available from spring

Besides the vegetables grown throughout the year and those coming into season, there are still some spring vegetables available, such as:

- arugula (rocket)
- asparagus
- beet (beetroot) greens
- carrots
- green beans
- scallions (spring onions)
- zucchini (courgettes)

A source of water

Like adults, children need to drink to keep healthy and keep growing. Water helps children's brains and body work properly and helps digestion. Encourage children to drink water each day so that they get into the habit.

The water in vegetables accounts for up to 95 percent of their weight —a valuable source of hydration. However, this water content makes vegetables prone to drying out, which is why it is important to use them quickly after harvesting. In particular, this loss of water also leads to loss of vitamins, minerals, and flavor.

Fall (Autumn)

The ripe and rich flavors of fall (autumn) vegetables are perfect for making soups, risotto dishes, and creams, in addition to pies and casseroles. All are a delicious way of bringing little ones into contact with the wonderful offerings of the season, and encouraging them to enjoy new experiences with food.

Broccoli

Broccoli, which comes in a wide range of types, is mainly grown in the center and south of Italy. Harvesting begins in the fall (autumn) and continues through late spring. Broccoli has few calories and is a source of vitamin C and B9 (folate). It also provides a good amount of dietary fiber, pro-vitamin A carotenoids, and magnesium. It has recently been shown to have interesting properties that may contribute to the prevention of certain cancers.

Buying and storing:
The best specimens have compact, firm, bright green florets and large and delicate leaves. Broccoli is quite hardy. If placed in a vegetable storage bag, it will keep in the crisper drawer of your refrigerator for more than a week.

Basic cooking:
Broccoli is best divided into florets and steamed for 10–15 minutes. Steaming results in the broccoli losing only 20 percent of its valuable antioxidants, while more conventional boiling will cause it to lose 70 percent. Boiling also makes it more difficult to digest.

Garbanzo beans (chickpeas) and lentils

Together with beans, garbanzo beans (chickpeas) and lentils are the most popular legumes or pulses. They are available dried in the late fall (autumn). They provide high biological value protein and contain amino acids lacking in cereal protein, making legumes and cereals complementary foods. The more contemporary way of eating pulses, such as in a simple pasta dish with beans, is a valid alternative to animal protein. They are a good source of dietary fiber, B-group vitamins, and minerals, particularly iron.

Buying and storing:
Good quality dried beans, peas, and lentils come in regular shapes with bright colors and a smooth surface. Store in a dry place away from light, and use within a year.

Basic cooking:
Dried garbanzo beans must be soaked in cold water for between 8 and 24 hours, while lentils don't need to be soaked. Boil for 1 hour or until tender.

Onions

Available throughout the year, onions were already highly prized by the ancient Egyptians before they were introduced into Europe by the Greeks. Besides being categorized by shape, color, and size, onions are also classified by when they are harvested. Onions harvested in winter are destined for storage. Onions contain large amounts of vitamins and minerals. They stimulate digestion and the metabolism, and supply beneficial antioxidants

Buying and storing:
Onions should be firm and compact, without shoots. Stored at room temperature in a dry and well-ventilated place away from light, they will keep for two to three weeks, until they begin to sprout.

Basic cooking:
Onions are an ingredient of countless dishes. They are delicious cooked in soups and omelets, and form a vital part of a soffritto—an aromatic mix of finely chopped onion, carrot, and celery that has been slowly fried in olive oil—which forms the basis of many recipes in this book.

Potatoes

New potatoes are harvested before they're fully grown, from March through to late July, while storage potatoes come onto the market in the fall (autumn). The many different varieties are mainly classified by the color of their flesh, because they have a different use depending on whether they're yellow or white. Potatoes are low in calories but provide a good amount of protein and dietary fiber. Their high potassium content make them particularly suitable for the diet of active people who engage in sport.

Buying and storing:
Well-stored, quality potatoes have healthy, shiny, and very soft skin, shallow eyes, and firm flesh, without patches of green. Unless treated with a sprout inhibitor, which should be stated on the label, potatoes will keep for a couple of months in winter in a cool and dark place to prevent the appearance of toxic shoots.

Basic cooking:
Peel, rinse, and cut each potato into quarters. Put into a pan, cover with at least 2 in (5 cm) of water, bring to a boil, cover with a lid, and continue to cook for 20 minutes to until tender. Mash the potatoes with a potato masher or for a chunkier texture, crush the potatoes with a fork.

Pumpkin and squash

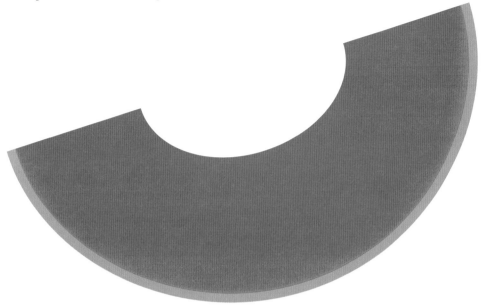

Native to Central America, the pumpkin was introduced into Europe in the sixteenth century. There are many varieties of pumpkin and squash, distinguished by their color, size, and appearance. With traditional round pumpkins, the small ones are sweeter and less fibrous; squashes come in all shapes and sizes, but good ones include the butternut squash and acorn squash.

The sweet and compact flesh of the pumpkin and squash, like all orange vegetables, is high in antioxidant carotenoids, which have cell-protecting antioxidant properties and can be used by the body to make vitamin A, which helps to keep the skin and immune system healthy.

Buying and storing:
Look for a pumpkin that makes a hollow sound when knocked. Its stem should be soft and firmly attached, and its skin unbruised. If sold in pieces, the flesh should be firm and brightly colored, and the seeds moist and slippery. A whole pumpkin will keep for two to four months in a cool place. Pieces of pumpkin will keep for a few days covered in plastic wrap, or for several months in a food storage bag in the freezer.

Basic cooking:
Peel the pumpkin or squash and cut it into small pieces. Put the pieces into a non-stick pan, and cover with either water or formula milk. Bring to the boil, cover with a lid, and continue to cook over a medium heat until the pumpkin or squash starts to break down, about 10 minutes. Add a few tablespoons of water if needed. Using a hand-held immersion (stick) blender or food processor, puree until smooth. The flesh can be cooked in a skillet (frying pan) and added to vegetable soup and risotto dishes.

Coming into season in fall (autumn):

- broccoli
- garbanzo beans (chickpeas) and lentils
- fennel
- Jerusalem artichoke
- mushrooms
- onions
- potatoes
- pumpkin
- radicchio

Still available from summer

Besides the vegetables grown throughout the year and those coming into season, there are still some summer vegetables available, such as:

- apricots
- bell peppers
- cavolo nero
- cucumbers
- eggplant (aubergine)
- peaches
- strawberries
- Swiss chard
- tomatoes
- zucchini (courgettes)

Endless supply of antioxidants

Vegetables contain large amounts of antioxidant vitamins and minerals, such as vitamin E, vitamin C, zinc, and selenium.

Other plant molecules present in vegetables also have this property, including anthocyanins, natural pigments in vegetables that are predominantly reddish purple in color; the flavones present in cabbage and onions; and the phytoestrogens that all vegetables contain.

Winter

Crisp, hardy, and packed with valuable nutrients, winter vegetables often have robust textures and flavors that children do not always appreciate. However, when carefully chosen and cleverly cooked, even picky young palates that are unwilling to experiment can be won over.

Artichoke

Eaten in ancient times, the artichoke was introduced into the West by the Arabs, and there are records of its cultivation in Europe dating back to the late fifteenth century.

Spiny-leaved varieties are available from November through to May, which are followed by the smoother spring varieties. Among the many winter varieties, the most common is the Violetta artichoke, which is oval and elongated in shape; the globe artichoke, with soft flesh and a more rounded shape; and the purple Tuscan artichoke, which is quite small and flavorful.

Artichokes are high in iron and a good source of this valuable mineral, provided they are seasoned with fresh lemon juice, as the vitamin C in the juice facilitates the absorption of iron.

Buying and storing:
Fresh artichokes are evenly colored and firm, with spiny "leaves," which are technically bracts, tightly bunched and with a closed tip, a long and hard stem, and fresh leaves. They can be stored like a bunch of flowers, with the stems immersed in water, for several days. Cleaned, well-dried, and sealed in a vegetable storage bag, they will keep in the refrigerator for at least five days. Once cooked, however, they must be eaten immediately because they tend to develop toxic compounds.

Basic cooking:
Choose only very tender artichokes. They are delicious sautéed, fried, or boiled.

Cabbage

Although available throughout the year, cabbage is actually a typical winter vegetable. The common white cabbage has layers of smooth and thick leaves forming a large rose, while the spring cabbage is tightly packed to form a light green or reddish-purple ball. The leaves of the Savoy cabbage, on the other hand, are dark green and wrinkled. Other very common varieties are cavolo nero, also known as Italian kale, with long leaves, and Brussels sprouts, which are actually leaf buds that grow over a tall stalk.

All cabbages, together with cauliflower and broccoli, belong to the family of cruciferous vegetables, and are high in vitamins A and C.

Buying and storing:
When buying cabbage, it should have a fresh and compact appearance, with fleshy leaves, bright color and delicate smell. It will keep in the refrigerator, tightly sealed in a vegetable storage bag, for more than one week.

Basic cooking:
Cabbage can be boiled before pureeing for babies, or sautéing in a skillet (frying pan), or added to soups.

Cauliflower

Depending on the variety, cauliflower can look like a large white, green, or purple flower head.

Like all cruciferous vegetables, cauliflower is high in potassium, folic acid, dietary fiber, calcium, iron, phosphorous, vitamin C, and compounds that protect from certain cancers.

Buying and storing:
Fresh cauliflower has a dense head of florets, free of browning, with fresh, outer leaves wrapped around the head that snap when broken. It will keep in the refrigerator, tightly sealed in a vegetable storage bag, for more than one week.

Basic cooking:
The best way of preparing cauliflower while keeping its nutritional properties intact is to steam it whole for no longer than 20 minutes, or when divided into florets for 10–12 minutes. Boiling in water isn't recommended because a large proportion of the vitamins are lost and it becomes more difficult to digest.

Leek

There are two main leek varieties grown. The first is a smaller leek that is harvested in spring, and the other is a larger leek, ripening in winter.

Leeks contain a type of fiber, know as prebiotic fiber that is particularly good at encouraging the growth of beneficial gut bacteria. Besides being a good source of dietary fiber, leek contains sulphur compounds that many have anti-inflammatory benefits.

Buying and storing:
Look for whole, straight leeks that are very white and firm. The leaves should be taut, thick, and snap when broken, and the roots should be firmly attached. Leeks will keep in the refrigerator for several days with the tops of the leaves covered. Once cooked, eat immediately.

Basic cooking:
The white part can be finely sliced and steamed, or sautéed in a skillet (frying pan). The tenderest part of the green section can be used to make soups and creams.

Radicchio

Depending on when the harvest falls, radicchio varieties are classified as either early (available in October and November) or Tardivo, the Italian for "late" (available from December through February).

There are many different varieties, including Rosso di Treviso, Rosso di Verona, and Rosso di Chioggia, and the variegated Castelfranco and Chioggia radicchio. Radicchio contains dietary fiber, folic acid, vitamin C, calcium, and potassium.

Buying and storing:
The best specimens have fleshy, brightly colored leaves in a compact but slightly open head. Radicchio will keep for one week in the refrigerator if tightly sealed in a vegetable storage bag or wrapped in a damp cloth. The Tardivo variety is hardier and will keep for a slightly longer time.

Basic cooking:
Radicchio can be broiled (grilled), or sautéed in a skillet (frying pan).

Coming into season in winter:

- broccoli rabe (rapini)
- Brussels sprouts
- butternut squash
- cauliflower
- clementines
- endive (chicory)
- escarole
- globe artichokes
- kale
- leeks
- radicchio
- rhubarb
- Savoy cabbage
- swedes
- sweet potatoes
- turnips

Still available from fall (autumn)

Besides the vegetables grown throughout the year and those coming into season at the point of winter, there are still some fall (autumnal) vegetables available, such as:

- apples
- beets (beetroot) and beet greens (beetroot tops)
- broccoli
- cabbage
- celeriac
- celery
- fennel
- lettuce
- parsnips
- pears
- pumpkin
- radicchio
- Swiss chard

Super fiber

Vegetables contain a great deal of dietary fiber, which improves intestinal transit, or the time it takes for food to pass through the body. But that is not all it does. Dietary fiber lines the intestinal walls with a protective gel that slows down the absorption of bile salts, cholesterol, and other harmful substances.

Taking waste into account

Before cooking, fresh vegetables need to be trimmed and often peeled, meaning that part will be discarded. This is an important factor to consider when calculating the quantity of vegetables to buy and calculating their real price by weight. Below is the average amount of wastage for each vegetable:

- asparagus – 30%
- carrots – 6%
- scallions (spring onions) – 20%
- beet greens – 6%
- green beans – 5%
- peas – 50%
- arugula (rocket) – 3%
- spinach – 17%
- sugar snap peas – 4%
- zucchini (courgette) – 3%

Index

Index

Recipe notes

Recommendations concerning infant nutrition vary from country to country. If you are concerned about any of the advice, recipes, or ingredients included in this book, please refer to your pediatrician for guidance.

Butter is always unsalted, unless otherwise specified.

Milk is always pasteurized and full-fat (whole), unless otherwise specified.

Eggs are assumed to be medium size, unless otherwise specified, and preferably organic and free-range. Eggs should always be thoroughly cooked when prepared for a baby.

All herbs are fresh, unless otherwise specified.

Individual fruits and vegetables, such as onions and pears, are assumed to be medium sized, unless otherwise specified, and should be peeled and/or washed.

Fish are always cleaned, gutted, and with all bones removed.

Ham means cooked ham, unless otherwise specified.

Do not add salt or sugar to food being prepared for a baby.

Do not add honey to food being prepared for a baby until they are at least 12 months old.

Cooking and preparation times are for guidance only, as individual ovens vary. If using a convection oven, follow the manufacturer's directions concerning oven temperatures.

Exercise a high level of caution when following recipes involving any potentially hazardous activity including the use of high temperatures and open flames.

All spoon and cup measurements are level, unless otherwise specified.

1 teaspoon = 5 ml
1 tablespoon = 15 ml

Australian standard tablespoons are 20 ml, so Australian readers are advised to use 3 teaspoons in place of 1 tablespoon when measuring small quantities.

Cup, metric, and imperial measurements are given in this book. Follow one set of measurements throughout, not a mixture, as they are not interchangeable.

Phaidon Press Limited
Regent's Wharf
All Saints Street
London N1 9PA

Phaidon Press Inc.
65 Bleecker Street
New York, NY 10012

phaidon.com

First published in English 2020
© 2020 Phaidon Press Limited

The recipes in this book are adapted from
Il grande cucchiaino d'argento: Le ricette
che piacciono ai bambini, published in 2018.
The first English edition of The Silver Spoon
was published by Phaidon in 2005. First
published in Italian by Editoriale Domus as
Il cucchiaio d'argento 1950. Eighth edition
(revised, expanded, and redesigned) 1997.
© Editoriale Domus S.p.A.

ISBN 978 1 83866 057 4

A CIP catalogue record for this book is
available from the British Library and the
Library of Congress.

Commissioning Editor: Emilia Terragni
Project Editor: Lisa Pendreigh
Production Controller: Rebecca Price

Design and Illustrations by Julia Hasting

Printed in China

The Publishers would also like to thank Tracey
Smith, João Mota, Angela Dowden, Ellie Smith,
Ellie Levine, Jo Ireson, Vanessa Bird, and Albino
Tavares for their contributions to the book.

Recipes adapted and tested by Amanda Grant

Amanda is a food writer, broadcaster, and
mother of Ella, Lola, and Finley. She has
published several books about healthy eating
for children, including The Silver Spoon for
Children, writes the Junior Cooks pages for
Delicious magazine, and is passionate about
teaching children about good food and how
to cook.

Illustrated by Julia Hasting

Julia Hasting is a graphic designer with an
international reputation for designing highly
engaging, conceptually refined, and uniquely
crafted books. For nearly two decades, she
has been Creative Director of Phaidon where
her design approach has set a new industry
standard. Her work has earned numerous
international design awards. In 2000 she
became an elected member of the Alliance
Graphique Internationale (AGI).